"This is a difficult book to read, thus I can only imagine how difficult it was to write. The wounds still seep. The aches still sear. The cries still rattle. Such is the experience of many who sit upon the ash heap of disillusioned faith. Faith in God has been found wanting in the light of abusive infidelity enacted upon the vulnerable by religious leaders and a global pandemic that has been politicized by those desperately clinging to power. It is so easy to walk away from faith, from community, from God. Many have. Many more will. Yet this book is not about deconstruction, for that is only part of the process of crafting a faith that will survive—no, *thrive*—in times when hope is merely a flickering ember. This is about the hard process of *reconstructing* faith, of punching through the dark and screaming with all one's might into the ether—praying, begging, for God to hear and come near. If this is you, I humbly invite you to read these words. My friend Tiffany has been where you are and has come through to the other side. In her, you will find a compassionate friend, a gentle guide, a kindred spirit."

— **Rob O'Lynn**
associate professor of preaching and ministry,
director of Graduate Bible programs, and dean of the School of
Distance and General Education at Kentucky Christian University

"Tiffany Yecke Brooks puts a new spin on an old problem—that problem being the seeming lack of compassion by Christians who the public assumes should be more compassionate than most. Those who are less familiar with God's Word sometimes construe Christian attitudes as if they belong to God. This projection causes anxiety about who God is and whether or not they can trust their own relationship with God. The topics brought up will make some uncomfortable, but, in the end, God comes out a winner. Brooks's comments are thought-provoking and hopefully conversation-provoking as well. A good read."

— **Cheryl Durham**
dean of students at Master's International University of Divinity

Gaslighted by God

RECONSTRUCTING
A DISILLUSIONED FAITH

TIFFANY YECKE BROOKS

WILLIAM B. EERDMANS PUBLISHING COMPANY
GRAND RAPIDS, MICHIGAN

Wm. B. Eerdmans Publishing Co.
4035 Park East Court SE, Grand Rapids, Michigan 49546
www.eerdmans.com

28 27 26 25 24 23 22   1 2 3 4 5 6 7

ISBN 978-0-8028-7868-7

Library of Congress Cataloging-in-Publication Data

Names: Brooks, Tiffany Yecke, author.
Title: Gaslighted by God : reconstructing a disillusioned faith /
    Tiffany Yecke Brooks.
Description: Grand Rapids, Michigan : William B. Eerdmans Pub-
    lishing Company, 2022. | Includes bibliographical references and
    index. | Summary: "A book for those who have experienced the
    spiritual trauma of fundamentalist Christianity, in which the
    author shows how a more authentic faith can be raised from the
    ashes of disillusionment"—Provided by publisher.
Identifiers: LCCN 2021043901 | ISBN 9780802878687
Subjects: LCSH: Fundamentalism. | God (Christianity) | Chris-
    tianity—Essence, genius, nature. | BISAC: RELIGION / Christian
    Living / Spiritual Growth | PSYCHOLOGY / Psychopathology /
    Post-Traumatic Stress Disorder (PTSD)
Classification: LCC BT82.2 .B75 2022 | DDC 270.8/2—dc23
LC record available at https://lccn.loc.gov/2021043901

CONTENTS

THIS IS NOT A BOOK ABOUT THAT

On November 29, 1961, *Mercury-Atlas 5* was launched from Cape Canaveral, Florida. "Manned" only by Enos the chimp, it was the first time the United States had successfully managed to launch a primate into orbital flight.

Enos's mission was simple: complete a series of tests for which he had trained more than 1,250 hours to prepare him for weightlessness and understanding basic on-screen commands. One of these tests was an "avoidance conditioning" exercise in which Enos pulled the correct lever to indicate which shape in a series of three was different. If he got the answer correct, he moved on to the next sequence of three; if he was incorrect, he received an electric shock to his feet. Enos underwent intensive training in this exercise to prepare for his mission.

The point of the experiment was to evaluate the effects of space flight on mental cognition, and Enos did his job admirably. All seemed promising for his mission to continue exactly as hoped, demonstrating that primates could in fact continue to operate at full intellectual capacity even in zero gravity.

But then, during orbit, something went horribly wrong. The equipment malfunctioned, and no matter what lever he pulled, Enos continued to receive shocks to his feet—thirty-three in a row. When that battery of tests was completed, he executed his other tasks perfectly fine until the avoidance conditioning test came up again. This time, with the glitch still in place, Enos received forty-one consecutive shocks.

To the amazement of the scientists and handlers on the ground, Enos doggedly continued his futile attempts to complete the task exactly as he had been trained by pulling the lever for the out-of-place graphic. "Certainly, following a malfunction of this nature, it might be expected that behavior would be disrupted," the official NASA report read afterward, "but this was not in evidence."

Enos's mission was supposed to be three complete orbits of Earth, but due to the equipment problems and an overheating issue in the capsule, he was brought back after completing only two. Then came the coup de grâce: Enos's craft landed in the Atlantic Ocean, south of Bermuda and miles off-target. The chimp was stranded, strapped inside the hot, cramped pod, bobbing helplessly in the ocean for almost three and a half hours until the USS *Stormes* was able to locate and retrieve him. It was this final insult that finally broke Enos. The obedient, tenacious chimp, who had dutifully completed his tasks despite receiving more than seventy electric shocks, snapped. When the capsule was opened at last by the rescue crew, the NASA report notes that "The subject had broken through the protective belly panel and had removed or damaged most of the physiological sensors. He had also forcibly removed the urinary catheter while the balloon was still inflated."[1]

How many of us have ever felt like Enos? We do everything we have been trained to do, and even when the system fails, we continue to carry out our work dutifully *because that is who we are.* We know the rules and we know what is expected of us. We understand that even though it's not always going to be easy, there will be delivery from our trials.

But then something goes haywire; the shocks don't stop, and our rescue doesn't seem to come. When we are finally face-to-face with the One in charge, we absolutely lose all composure and rage against the inherent unfairness of the setup. We did our job, but something was broken, and we ended up getting punished—over and over and over again—because the people in power made a mistake that harmed us. This was not the deal we were promised.

Enos's story is heartbreaking for many reasons, but perhaps mostly because of his response to the circumstances beyond his control. His destruction of the capsule and his injury to himself are deeply understandable; after all, he had played his part, faithfully doing exactly what he had been trained was the right thing to do—even when it cost him dearly. But he reached a breaking point, and he reverted from a meticulously trained human stand-in back to a wild animal. And who could blame him? He had persevered, despite the constant punishment he received for doing the right thing. But at some point, his will and his resolve were pushed past their limits by circumstances beyond his control or comprehension.

◦ ◦ ◦

This is not a book about blindly trusting an all-loving God, no matter the situation or circumstances.

This is not a book about perseverance and fighting the good fight.

This is not a book about "More of Thee and less of me."

This is not a book about that.

This book is the friend who crawls into the ashes to sit with you without telling you to count your blessings.

This is a book designed to offer companionship, not sermons.

This is a book to help you feel seen, heard, and less alone.

This is a book to help you give a shape and a name to the emotions you might be trying to convince yourself you aren't really feeling.

One of the major trends in current marriage and family therapy graduate programs is systems theology, in which people are
encouraged to identify their role in the function and dysfunction
of their family or social system. People are encouraged to identify
their contribution to the conflict in an effort to avoid martyrdom
or the blame game. This approach can be helpful—to a point. The
problem with such a philosophy is that it can easily be twisted
into injured people asking themselves, "What did I do to deserve
to be belittled/humiliated/harassed/assaulted/abused/violated/
falsely accused/controlled/cheated on/neglected?" Even though
such thinking is clearly not the intention, it is an easy trap for a
broken, exhausted person to fall into—especially if that person
has been brought up to believe in divine correction, discipline, or
interference in every minute aspect of life. What is more, the tools
of systematic theology in the hands of untrained church leaders
can be a slippery slope to victim blaming and victim shaming.

Too often, we parrot ideas we have not examined critically
because we are more desperate to help God "save face" to un-
believers than we are to engage in honest dialogue that can get
sticky, awkward, and difficult. We often hear about the unknowable ways of God that have nothing to do with our own goodness or evil, while in the next breath we simply substitute the
word "consequences" for *karma*: "You made mistakes, and you
are being punished for them. That's how consequences work."
Or, even more simply, we just chalk it up to "the wages of sin."
It does much less damage to our comfortable theology to pin the
blame on the person rather than on a supposedly benevolent and
all-powerful God. And heaven forbid we admit that God doesn't
always meet our expectations.

With the strong emphasis that many religious and inspirational
circles place on personal responsibility and "empowerment thinking," many of us have been discouraged from seeing ourselves as
victims even in situations where we are not at fault. In our determination to embrace spiritual maturity, rise above circumstances, and

gain wisdom from difficult experiences, we push ourselves to make meaning from such events: "This happened because God needed me to learn _____." While this can be true in many cases, in others we are essentially pleading guilty to crimes we didn't commit.

In an effort to exonerate God, many religious leaders have twisted biblical texts to pin the blame on the individual. It is time to reassert the simple truths that bad things happen to good people and life is not fair—*and that may not be your fault.* It is time to be honest about the fact that a person can be morally virtuous and still face profound injustice or misfortune. It is time to acknowledge that the God of our experience might not align with the God we were taught to see in Scripture. It is time to reclaim our *experience* of God.

o o o

This is not a book of easy answers. The discussions in the coming pages are not designed to give you simple talking points or the proverbial "spiritual shot in the arm." There are few, if any, Scriptures that offer a straightforward prescription on how to respond to this sort of faith crisis.

This is not a book about how to push beyond questioning or struggling or even doubting; there are countless other books that already fill that space.

This is not a book about troubles that are "light and momentary" or about how to deal with disappointment or how to buck up after a setback.

This is not a book about the kind of hurt made better by a good night's sleep. This is about the repeated blows, the kicks while you are down, the salt in the wound as you try to do what God has asked of you.

This is not a book for people who are asking for permission to be disenchanted with faith or who are wondering whether it's okay to be angry with God; it's for people who are already there, whether it's okay or not.

This is not another book about how pain is part of a fallen world but God is bigger than the pain.

This is not another book about how we just need to pray a little more.

This is not another book about the refiner's fire or Jesus calming storms.

This is not a book that denies the reality of sin.

This is not a book that says consequences aren't real.

This is not a book that imagines that real-world decisions don't have spiritual implications and vice versa.

This is not another book about how we are all somehow "doing church wrong" in twenty-first-century, middle-class America.

This is also not a "burn book" about all the ways that God has failed us, or belief is a joke, or religion is meaningless in the modern world.

This is not a book about any of that.

This is a book for people asking, "How do I make sense of this uncharted territory that Sunday school and Christian media never prepared me to face?"

This is a book for people who are well past the point of questioning, "Is it okay if I am angry with God?" and are instead wondering, "What do I do with that anger?"

This is a book about soul-crushing, life-altering pain and injustice—over and over again—as you persist in following the Lord.

This is a book for people who are tired of being told that the immense, all-encompassing pain in their life is somehow something they deserve.

This is a book for people who refuse to explain away the God they have personally encountered with Scriptures that paint a different picture.

This book is designed to be a companion, a voice of reassurance that you are not alone in your experiences or your emotions. It is intended to help you find honest labels for your "problematic" thoughts and feelings rather than deny them in broad strokes of "Christianese" or certain acceptable sayings that collapse under scrutiny.

This is a book of sympathy more than a book of suggestions, because simplified, generic advice rarely addresses the real, gaping complexities of a specific situation.

This is a book that, I hope, will reassure you that there *can* be faith during and after periods of trial, emptiness, and anger. That new faith may not look like the kind you grew up with—in fact, it almost certainly won't—but it will be a faith born of genuine experience and testing of God rather than purely philosophical ideas and superficial clichés. It will be a faith that is bruised, battered, nuanced, and *real*, rather than one wrapped in tissue-thin platitudes and three-point sermons that hold firmly to the party line.

This is a book for those who, like Enos, have followed the rules, done their best, completed the tasks asked of them—*even though the rules changed*—and are currently fumbling with the zipper and snaps to throw off their space suits and announce, "That's it! I'm done with all of this mess!" In fact, I'll admit that, for a hot second, I seriously considered calling this book *Space Chimps for God*, but I quickly realized that monkeys in space suits don't quite capture the magnitude of the subject.

Because this is a serious topic and a major problem. And, chances are, if you picked up this book, you are facing a crisis of faith, a crucible moment, a Dark Night of the Soul. And when you are surrounded by darkness, it can be hard to perceive anyone or anything around you with certainty.

This is a book about how we renegotiate our understanding of a God who no longer seems good and who no longer seems godly—a God who seems to have broken all the rules.

This is a book for people who know that what they are being asked to shoulder is more than they signed up for.

This is a book for people who are fed up with pat answers and bad theology.

This is a book about shedding unnecessary shame and freeing yourself to meet the Almighty as you are authentically experiencing God, not as you have been told you *should* experience God.

This is a book about you. This is a book about me. This is a book about how we can navigate these terrifying and unfamiliar waters together, however long that takes.

This is a book about understanding that the God who waits for us on the other side may look completely different from the God we thought we knew, but that does not mean God has changed. It means we are seeing God with different eyes.

1

SHELL-SHOCKED FAITH:
RECONCILING SCRIPTURE AND EXPERIENCE

Matthew 16:13–20

With the dawn of World War I, an entire generation of young British men left for the battlefields carrying two things: a newfangled Lee-Enfield bolt action, magazine-fed repeating rifle and an education that was steeped in the classics—most notably, Homer's epic of honor and empire, *The Iliad*. From the poshest boarding schools to the humblest country classrooms, study of Greek and Roman literature was the backbone of the educational system of the largest empire in human history. These young men had been raised on the promises of the glory of war; it was what made a man a man and conquered the globe. Nothing could be nobler than charging into battle, wielding a sword for king and country and the unshakable belief that God was on the side of the Crown.

But World War I was not like the legendary battles of which old men and politicians spoke so proudly. It was not like any war the world had ever seen. Whereas before a person had to look the enemy in the eye as they clashed swords or fired muskets at relatively close range, now, for the first time, modern war machines like

tanks, machine guns, and even airplanes could mow down an entire battalion anonymously. Chlorine and mustard gas could blind,
maim, or kill an entire battlefield in a matter of minutes. Soldiers
went from men on a mission to mechanized automatons with all
humanity stripped from them by this new technology. Never mind
which side God was on; the more pressing question was whether,
in the midst of the carnage and misery, God existed at all.

Every golden promise of glorious battle shattered in the
machine-gun fire or rotted in the trenches. And it wasn't just the
British; disillusionment with the empty promises of an outdated
system echoed through the allied ranks and even across enemy
lines. The literature of the era reflects this plainly in the haunted
memories of so many of Ernest Hemingway's protagonists, in the
horrors of the trenches and mental anguish of returning soldiers
in Erich Maria Remarque's *All Quiet on the Western Front*, and in the
chilling lines of Wilfred Owen's battlefield poems such as "Dulce et
Decorum Est" and "Anthem for a Doomed Youth," published post-
humously after Owen was killed in battle in November 1918, just one
week before the armistice. An entire generation was disenchanted
by the lie they had been sold about the nobility and glory of war.

Soldiers who survived the trenches often faced "shell shock."
What we now understand as a serious medical condition called
post-traumatic stress disorder was then often regarded as a character flaw or a sign of mental weakness; its sufferers were sometimes even classified as social deviants. Instead of being treated
with compassion, many shell-shocked soldiers were faced with
only two choices: get back out on the battlefield or face charges
of cowardice. The fear was that shell shock could be contagious,
and if one soldier became confused, stunned, or unable to carry
out orders to a T, others would follow suit. The entire battle could
be lost because one person didn't buck up and toe the line.

Veterans who came home emotionally broken were written
off as weak, lacking mettle, or as mentally disturbed. They didn't
look the way the leaders wanted their returning heroes to look

because these battle-weary veterans didn't fit the golden narrative that political PR machines had sold the public. In some cases, these victims lived fragile, hidden lives where they were largely regarded with a mixture of curiosity, fear, and disdain. Others found that their experiences in the war left them alienated from people and places they once called home, so they left to establish thriving communities with other expatriates. Collectively, they were eventually dubbed "the Lost Generation" for their struggles to reintegrate into a society that was naïve, or even willfully ignorant, about the real-life struggles, questions, doubts, abuses, and horrors they had endured. And with the shattered pieces of the world they thought they once knew, this lost generation built a movement called modernism.

o o o

That is where many, many Christians and former Christians are right now. Some people endure hell in the trenches and emerge with a deeper faith. Some people find God in the ashes and the rubble. And some people get shell-shocked by life because the promise and the reality don't align, and how do you make meaning of the world after that? How do you step back into life when the world you thought you knew has proven itself fundamentally different—darker, more chaotic, less certain—than everything upon which you built your belief? How do you find your place in a body of believers that discounts your experiences? Shell shock is not the result of cowardice but of exposure—of bravely facing the trauma again and again until it takes its toll. When good people feel rejected by the very institution that first provided their ethical foundation, they may necessarily turn outward to make meaning of their experiences. This is where we begin to hear conversations about "faith deconstruction" and "compassionate humanism." Usually, the desire is not to renounce morality altogether but simply to figure out how to live as decent human beings, apart from the structure or safety net of an organized religion that has deemed them misguided, less than, or damaged. Many (probably most) people who separate from formal Christianity don't do it to chase a hedonistic lifestyle full of orgies and Satanism; what they want instead is to figure out how to shed the man-made parts of religion while clinging to the sacred and the divine. They want to be good people without the cultural hang-ups and "branding problems" of the modern church. It's almost like spiritual downsizing, where you drop the excess, the bloat, the unnecessary clutter, and the trappings of materialism, to focus instead only on the basics of what you actually need and love for a meaningful and more focused life.

◦ ◦ ◦

Despite all the dire warnings from the pulpit and across Christian airwaves about "postmodern Christianity," where anything goes, truth means nothing, and even the existence of God is questionable, the reality is that most of us are not nearly so ready to throw away *all* aspects of belief. We are much more like the modernists following World War I. Our understanding of the world was damaged beyond repair; we can't go back to the life we once knew and pretend not to have seen and heard and felt everything we experienced. But neither are we willing to turn our backs on God completely. We are trying to pick up the shattered pieces of our faith and reassemble them into some kind of mosaic that makes sense—that keeps the basic elements and the truths without replicating the old patterns that didn't survive the war. This isn't a *de*construction as so many fear-mongering religious leaders have declared; it is a *re*construction. We are fishing fragments of our religious worldview out of the mud and piecing together something like Christianity. It takes more faith to stay and try to make sense of the shards than it does to simply walk away from the rubble. And anyone who insists that such a drastic reconstruction would never pass the "What Would Jesus Do?" test has clearly never paid attention to Matthew 5, when

Jesus repeats six times, "You have heard it said . . . but I say to you . . ." No matter how loudly the religious leaders protested or how strongly they pushed back, Jesus was undeterred from dismantling and reassembling the old structures and distorted beliefs present in his own cultural context to preach a gospel of love and acceptance.

o o o

In *A Moveable Feast*, Ernest Hemingway recounts the story of the now-famous line, "You are all a lost generation," and how it led to an argument between himself and his mentor, Gertrude Stein. She had told him how a young Parisian mechanic and war veteran had failed to repair her Model T to her exacting standards, and that the owner of the garage had sneered at his employee in French, "You are all a lost generation." Stein then turns the phrase to needle Hemingway and all the young people of his circle.

> "That's what you are, that's what you all are," Miss Stein said. "All of you young people who served in the war. You are a lost generation."
>
> "Really?" I said.
>
> "You are," she insisted. "You have no respect for any thing. . . . Don't argue with me, Hemingway," Miss Stein said. "It does no good at all. You're all a lost generation, exactly as the garage keeper said."
>
> Later when I wrote my first novel I tried to balance Miss Stein's quotation from the garage keeper with one from Ecclesiastes. But that night walking home I thought about the boy in the garage and if he had ever been hauled in one of those vehicles when they were converted to ambulances. I remembered how they used to burn out their brakes going down the mountain roads with a full load of wounded. . . . I thought of Miss Stein and Sherwood Anderson and egotism and mental laziness versus discipline and I thought who is calling who a

lost generation? . . . [T]he hell with her lost generation talk and
all the dirty, easy labels. (29-31)

Hemingway writes that he turned those words over and over
in his head that night, remembering his own experiences from
the war and wondering what the young French mechanic's were
like. Finally, he reaches the conclusion that people like the garage
owner and Stein and everyone else who was dismissive of Hemingway's generation—of their questioning, seeking, trauma, and
the disillusionment that lay under it all—were simply egotists.
They aren't governed by any kind of moral authority, despite what
they seem to think; they are merely convinced of their own superiority because they have never felt such disenchantment. They
levy judgment from their comfortable seats while knowing nothing of what life was actually like in the war. Hemingway finally
rejects every easy, lazy identifier those people wanted to stamp
on his generation because they never even bothered to consider
what he and his compatriots had endured both in the war and in
their homecoming that made them so "lost" in the first place.

This story strikes frighteningly close to home for many of
us. We went to spiritual war armed with cheery Sunday school
lessons and *I Kissed Dating Goodbye*, and we believed completely
in the promise that if we only followed the Bible and what the
preacher told us, we would end up with an abundant, beautiful
life. Yes, there might be trials, but God's people always came out
on top. There would always be an eleventh-hour miracle if one
just had enough faith.

Then we took our collection of Scriptures and evangelical zeal,
and we lived life in the trenches by those rules and promises,
and we stumbled home, limping, hurting, and shell-shocked,
to churches that had no place for us because we no longer fit
their narrative. When we tried to share our stories or voice our
traumas, we were shut down, told we were wrong, or charged
with cowardice. When we gathered up the courage to give voice

to our struggles, we were assigned labels: doubter, questioner, backslider, heretic, cherry picker, "anything goes" Christian.

These names are often slapped on by people with a very narrow set of life experiences and, consequently, a very narrow view of God. Maybe they've never questioned anything because they didn't have to. Maybe they've never doubted because they've never ventured far enough outside their comfort zone to experience pain deep enough to trigger disbelief. Whatever the case, they almost certainly never set foot in our war.

Like Hemingway, we shell-shocked believers often find ourselves wanting to challenge the critics: Have you been in the trenches with us? Have you navigated the roads we've navigated? Have you suffered our pain? Have you lived our war? Have you had to do faith triage on your life? Have you watched as your soul bled out? No? *Then spare us your judgment and condemnation.*

When you try to explain what it was like in the heat of the battle—the endless noise and confusion, the carnage of unanswered prayers, the shattering of every cherished belief you once held about the world—they only see the brokenness as a character flaw, not the wounds of a battle beyond their comprehension. And if those critics aren't listening to the people who *did* come staggering back, you can only imagine what they're thinking about the ones who didn't.

"There was no such thing as a lost generation. I thought beat-up, maybe, but damned if we were lost," Hemingway wrote to his biographer in 1951. The only ones who were truly lost, he argued, were the ones who died or went insane; the rest were merely unprepared for the realities of the world they inherited. "We were a very solid generation," he argued, "though without education (some of us)."[1]

That is you. That is us. We are beat-up, battered, perhaps even bitter, but not lost. We are survivors seeing things more clearly than we ever did before. In a world where the armistice may never come, we are attempting to rebuild our lives not according to the old, hypothetical ideas that couldn't stand up to the realities of war. We need something more solid than formulaic, catchall solutions. We need something rock hard—not just the simple answer of "Jesus," but of everything he stands for: love, mercy, grace, inclusion, humility, compassion—but also righteous anger at abuses of power, raw and honest emotion when we feel forsaken, and the freedom to challenge the religious leaders of our day who tell us that the things we know to be true are somehow wrong or even sinful because they do not fit into a very narrow and exacting definition of what is "right."

There are few things more frustrating than a phone call with customer service where the representative walks you through the proper steps to repair your device, and it still doesn't work:

"The green light should be on now."

"It's not."

"Try again."

"It's still not."

"But we followed every step in the manual. It has to be working. Are you sure it's not working? Check again. You're missing it."

"I did everything you told me to, multiple times. I'm the one sitting here, looking at the device. No lights are coming on."

"Well, you're mistaken. We followed the manual to the letter. It must be user error."

For those who grew up in evangelical churches, the acronym "Basic Instructions Before Leaving Earth" is likely familiar. There is no situation, we were assured, that could not be resolved by prayer and Bible study. The challenge comes when the promises laid out in Scripture don't seem to align with the experience of life. What should we trust: The words on the page or the reality of our situation? It's easy to tell people to have more faith, to pray more fervently, to be humbler, and to dive into the Word with extra devotion. But what do we do when James 4:8, "Draw near to God, and he will draw near to you,"[2] rings hollow? Too often, we hide our struggles or cover up our doubts because we fear they will damage our Christian witness. We pretend our anger or confusion isn't real. We don't express our frustration honestly for fear of being preached at, rejected, or having our experiences "church-splained" back to us in order to "correct" our perceptions.

Most of us are familiar with the term "gaslighting," taken from the 1938 play *Gas Light* by Patrick Hamilton that was later turned into a movie starring Ingrid Bergman. In the story, a woman is driven to the brink of madness by her conniving husband, whose stealthy activities cause the lighting in the house to increase and diminish; meanwhile, he denies anything of the sort is happening in order to gain control over her. In psychology, the term is used to apply to a form of emotional abuse wherein the victim is repeatedly told that certain events, behaviors, patterns, and experiences did not really happen the way the victim thinks they did. The result is a deep questioning of one's mental stability, confidence, and fundamental belief system.

For many modern Christians, this conflict of rhetoric versus experience creates a faith crisis when the language of belief and the nature of God we've been taught to understand seem insufficient to meet the complexities of our deepest trials. The truths we were told are absolute may actually be far more nuanced than we care to admit, but speaking honestly about them can result in isolation, shame, or loss of identity. It often seems that grace is extended to all things but questioning, and mercy to everyone but the doubter. The denial of authentic feelings and experiences that fall outside the "party line" of the church can lead to a deterioration and even a complete collapse of faith.

When we reject what we know to be true, we are engaging in gaslighting, trying to make ourselves believe that reality is false. If we cannot deny the truth of what we have experienced nor a fundamental belief in God—yet the two seem in conflict with one another—then there *must* be a reconciliation. But . . . how?

When our experience differs from what the Bible seems to be telling us, there are only three possible options:

1. The Bible is right, which means our experience is somehow wrong.
2. Our experience is right, which means the Bible is somehow wrong.
3. Our understanding or application of the Bible is somehow off-base, which means maybe we need to shift our thinking about God.

(More on the first option in a moment.) The second option is a dangerous step toward rejecting God altogether. The third option, however, allows us to humbly accept that there are simply things that humans cannot comprehend. But rather than moving forward in blind surrender without a single discerning thought or question, we engage with our faith in a dynamic way that makes room for growth, that allows our relationship with God to evolve, and that leaves room for nuance, mystery, and wonder.

Unfortunately, the most common answer many of us receive in our churches or hear in Christian programming is that first option, that the Bible is right—full stop, end of story. And if what we are experiencing seems to run counter to the promises we've been told are ours in Scripture, then the only possible explanation is that we aren't really experiencing what we are experiencing—that our reality is somehow wrong because something is wrong with *us*. When our reality does not align with the interpretation or agenda of a person in power, and the person tells us we are wrong, crazy, lying, stupid, flawed, broken, deceptive, not good enough—when the things we know to be true are discounted because they threaten someone else's authority or control—that is textbook gaslighting, plain and simple. And it is rampant in too many of our churches.

The point of this book is not to pick a fight with any one spiritual leader or denomination, or to air grievances of decades (or centuries) of bad theology that have warped the freedom of the gospel into a legalistic set of contractual agreements with God. The intention here is not to examine every way the modern church has somehow gotten it wrong or angrily name and denounce specific perpetrators of spiritual abuse. That is not to say that there is not a need for accountability—quite the opposite. But it is not the focus of this particular study. The goal is to offer a safe place to sit with anger, confusion, heartbreak, and "heretical" thoughts. It is a lifeline to believers who have been told their emotions are sinful and dangerous or their dissatisfaction with easy answers means they would be better off discarding their faith altogether. If any of the reframing suggestions in the coming pages seem too simplistic or do not encompass where you are, let them go. Though each chapter offers its own twist of the narrative, the truth is that sometimes the twist is that there is no twist. Sometimes there are no words to make a situation better, no reinterpreting that can provide balm for the soul. That's real, too. The whole point of this book is simply to acknowledge the reality of the reader's lived experience as a valid and essential part of their personal faith.

But why this title? It seems intentionally combative at best and heretical at worst to accuse God of gaslighting, don't you think?

Yes. That's exactly the point. This book is for those who are so broken down, so shell-shocked, so soul-tired that they can't bear the thought of picking up another book that tells them they need to pray more, study the Bible more, trust more, carry more guilt about their own sin—*then* maybe God will finally listen to them. This is about reconsidering, reinterpreting, rehabilitating, and sometimes reframing; it is not about repenting. This isn't a book that promises that if you just squeeze enough Jesus on a situation, it will get better.

The problem isn't God; it's the narrative we've constructed around God that too often utilizes language of abuse or manipulation. For centuries, various iterations of "We are nothing without God," "We will never be enough on our own," and "for such a worm as I" have been important relational terms within much of Protestantism. It is as if "humble yourself in the sight of the Lord" meant some bully in the sky wanted to humiliate and enslave us, not that we ought to feel awe and wonder in the presence of the Creator of the universe. The reason? People who do not see themselves as worthy of God's notice are less likely to challenge God's self-appointed gatekeepers who enjoy the power that comes with controlling who has access to grace, love, and acceptance. It is not God who has gaslighted us but people who have distorted the lens by which we see and understand God, and who would seek to shame us when we question such notions, and the systems that keep them in power.

It is not God who has gaslighted us but people who have distorted the lens by which we see and understand God, and who would seek to shame us when we question such notions and the systems that keep them in power.

When people of faith—the men and women who are supposed to be God's hands and feet in this world—tell you that your sincere questions, doubts, disappointments, and lived experience with God are somehow "wrong" because they do not align with someone else's interpretation of what a "biblical Christian walk" is supposed to look like, they are engaging in gaslighting, whether they mean to or not.

When adults in the church blame one group of people for the thoughts, choices, and behavior of another rather than encouraging personal responsibility and accountability, that is gaslighting.

When a radio preacher's first response to a caller is, "You need to get in there and fix your marriage" instead of asking, "Please tell me more about your circumstances," that is gaslighting.

When legalism traps people in abusive and dangerous relationships, that is gaslighting.

When people of faith wrap messages of hatred, exclusion, and rejection in a guise of love because "we want to save your soul from hell," that is gaslighting.

When religious leaders denigrate or demean one of their own on social media for daring to voice a contrary opinion, that is gaslighting.

When a missionary confuses cultural values with actual mandates from God, that is gaslighting.

When the gospel is wrapped in the national flag, or one group insists another can't bear the name "Christian" unless they vote in a certain way, that is gaslighting.

When church marquees reduce truth to a few zingers with little regard for deeper theological implications, that is gaslighting.

When a preacher insists that depression is a character flaw that flies in the face of God's grace or that mental health issues should be treated with prayer and Bible study rather than medication and therapy, that is gaslighting.

When we push a message of "sexual purity" so much that we reduce people to the value of their virginity and consign an entire generation to lives marked by shame, guilt, or sexual frustration, that is gaslighting.

When church leaders engage in sexual harassment or misconduct and publicly denounce their victims as liars or extortionists, that is gaslighting.

When we prioritize the ideas of marriage, family, modesty, gatekeeping, literalism, nationalism, being "right," being "countercultural," self-preservation, or anything else over the immediate physical, emotional, and spiritual needs of another human being, that is gaslighting.

When we use the Bible to convince hurting people that their honest, earnest struggle with God somehow makes them less worthy of love, fellowship, or a place at the table, *that is gaslighting.*

It's not our table; it's God's. We were not called to be the bouncers or the spiritual "mean girls" who keep people away. Our job is to welcome people, to make room, and to extend invitation, not to tell them why they can't sit there.

On the other hand, neither is it our job to gloss over anything hurtful and insist that the Christian walk is paved with joy. A "positive vibes only" approach to church means that people facing spiritual difficulties, doubt, or deconstruction cannot be honest about their struggles or risk exclusion or rejection; it creates an atmosphere many psychologists call "toxic positivity."[3] When did we decide as a church that sadness is somehow a moral failing? Our job is not to try to "love-bomb" the disappointment or anger out of hurting souls, but to hear their stories and bear witness to their pain. Pain at the soul level is rarely so simple or so shallow to be "cured" with a few pat answers. Slapping a couple of out-of-context Scriptures to a spiritual wound will barely stop the bleeding, let alone save the patient.

These ideas might sound dangerous or heretical to those fortunate enough never to have had to consider them, but it all comes down to engaging with the Almighty rather than following a paint-by-numbers faith. It is the difference between being able to replicate a recipe exactly and being able to cook an original dish from whatever you have on hand. When we understand the chemistry of each element—how one makes things rise and another causes ingredients to bind on a molecular level—we can create infinite edible dishes instead of simply trying to apply the same formula, over and over, to an ever-changing array of ingredients. In this way, we make our faith a feast to which we can invite others to join us.

This kind of faith reconstruction is not a means of justifying and indulging one's own choices without regard for God's teaching; it is extending compassion to ourselves and to others who have faced a battle for which they were wholly unprepared. True compassion—more than sympathy, empathy, or anything else—comes not from kindness or thoughtfulness as much as it comes from validating the pain of someone who feels powerless in a system, culture, or setting. Many people who advocate stances that may be perceived as victim blaming or faith shaming are not intentionally unkind or uncaring individuals; it's just that they may never have known what it is like to feel as if there is no hope or recourse in a major, life-changing situation. Too often, we try to determine a person's *motives* rather than paying attention to the *experiences* that have shaped their worldviews. Motives imply judgment; experiences imply wisdom. Powerlessness means there is no hope for recourse or hope; as Dante famously imagined inscribed over the gates of hell, "Abandon all hope, ye who enter here." Hell is a place of hopelessness, and hopelessness feels like hell for those who are trapped within it. That is what is at the heart of so much of Jesus's preaching that we modern Christians often struggle to understand: the majority of his audiences did not know how to interpret his teachings outside of a lens of powerlessness; many of us in the modern Western church don't know how to interpret them outside of a political system that at least claims to extend equal protections under the law. Too often, our churches are hitting people with rationalism when what they need is compassion. Our churches are giving their children snakes and scorpions when they asked for basic spiritual sustenance (Luke 11:11–12).

> *Too often, we try to determine a person's* motives *rather than paying attention to the* experiences *that have shaped their worldviews.*

There will be critics, of course, who argue that finding meaning from personal experience that does not perfectly align with a certain interpretation of Scripture is a violation of Proverbs 3:5:

> Trust in the LORD with all your heart,
>   and do not rely on your own insight.

Such lessons cannot be trusted, they may argue, because they grant too much leeway for questions, reinterpretations, and recognizing God in places that aren't the traditional structures around which modern Western Christianity is built. Any reliance on one's own interactions with God, they insist, is proof of the warning in 2 Timothy 4:3-4: "For the time is coming when people will not put up with sound doctrine, but having itching ears, they will accumulate for themselves teachers to suit their own desires, and will turn away from listening to the truth and wander away to myths." The naysayers may even point out that experience must be subdued in favor of Scripture, since Paul writes just one chapter earlier that "All Scripture is inspired by God and is useful for teaching, for reproof, for correction, and for training in righteousness, so that everyone who belongs to God may be proficient, equipped for every good work" (2 Tim. 3:16-17). In other words, the Bible has been pre-vetted; your personal interactions with God have not.

The Scriptures that can be wielded in such a discussion are myriad, and what better use for the Word of God than to negate, shut down, invalidate, or otherwise discount someone's lived experience, right?* Critics are sure to claim the arguments in this book are cherry-picked and will provide their own Scriptures to refute these ideas—as if those verses themselves have not been cherry-picked in rebuttal. Such arguments are ultimately (excuse

---

* Out of an abundance of caution, I feel compelled to assure any reader who isn't quite sure that this is *very definitely sarcasm.*

the pun) fruitless; any portion of Scripture is best understood in the broader context of the entire book, the culture in which it was produced, and the conditions under which it was preserved, re-copied, and translated. But such an exhaustively in-depth exam-ination of each and every passage is impossible in a normal dis-cussion. We all pick and choose the verses and stories that resonate with us and apply them as we see fit. Of course this book cherry-picks; so will its critics. It is impossible not to. The point here is not to dissect individual verses and apply any overturned theology to one's entire faith structure. The point is to consider a handful of ways in which God may seem to act contrary to the divine na-ture, and how flawed theology and flawed people may have led us to assumptions and beliefs that are far too limiting, exclusionary, blame oriented, manipulative, or otherwise damaging.

But this is not a "diet Christianity" or "faith lite" that is some-how devoid of nutritional value or substance; this is a faith for people who hunger and thirst for not only righteousness but also a more nuanced theology. Remember, the religious powers-that-be have always hurled accusations of heresy against those who be-lieve the common man or woman can interact directly with God; just ask John Wycliffe, Jan Hus, Joan of Arc, Martin Luther, Wil-liam Tyndale. . . . Sometimes, the only difference between a heretic and a saint is the direction in which the winds of history blow.

The Bible itself offers us very real examples of Jesus caring about someone's personal understanding. In Matthew 16, Jesus asks his disciples who people say the Son of Man is. They cite var-ious schools of thought, but none of them is quite right. Finally Jesus asks, "But who do you say that I am?"

Who do you say that I am?

*Who do **you** say that I am?*

Jesus didn't demand complete adherence to the opinions of the religious leaders or the popular interpretations of prophecy; he cared what his disciples thought. He cared what the real people—those who, day in and day out, were at his side and saw his works firsthand—believed about him. He wanted to know how their experiences of walking with him had changed their perspective and how seeing him in action had helped them understand God more fully. And when Peter answers, "You are the Messiah, the Son of the living God," Jesus does not rebuke him for coming to a conclusion rooted in his own experience; instead, he blesses Peter for such a rich and full understanding. Such insight was not the result of stubbornly adhering to other people's interpretations. Peter didn't reach that deduction by shutting down his own curiosity or powers of observation in favor of what he was told to believe. He spoke from a belief rooted in all he had seen and lived in his time serving Jesus, and Jesus tells him that the conclusions to which he came were sacred: "For flesh and blood has not revealed this to you, but my Father in heaven" (Matt. 16:17). As it turns out, God-breathed Scripture may not be the only place truth is revealed to us. Sometimes, God shows up in our own revelations, epiphanies, and interpretations.

This story—and the notably nonscriptural profession Peter makes, upon which Jesus declares, "I will build my church"— illustrates in no uncertain terms that our lived experience is an essential part of our theology and witness. God values our personal interactions with him just as much, if not more, than he does the blind parroting of the religious party line.

We see this truth in the Old Testament, as well. Proverbs 19:27 presents a challenge to translators because, in its most literal reading, it seems to be contradicting much of the rest of the book, which urges the listener not to reject wise teachings. In an attempt to bring this seemingly rogue statement in line with the rest of the book, many modern versions of the Bible present the passage as a conditional statement: "Stop listening to instruction, my son, and you will stray from the words of knowledge" (NIV) or "My son, if you stop listening to instruction, you will stray from the principles of knowledge" (ISV). But such readings make slight adjustments to the literal meaning of the Hebrew. Ironically, some of the less-exacting translations capture the literal sense of the passage better, letting it stand exactly as written rather than performing linguistic gymnastics to make it palatable: "Cease, my son, to hear the instruction that causeth [you] to err from the words of knowledge" (KJV) and "Stop listening to teaching that contradicts what you know is right" (TLB). When we take this proverb at face value, we see it is not out of line with the rest of the book at all; it's simply encouraging the reader not to feel beholden to teachings that run counter to common sense.

The goal of this book you are now holding is not to encourage you to reject your long-held beliefs but to help you to consider new ways of applying those beliefs that offer broader grace and spiritual freedom. The goal is not to root out all old ideas and toss them aside without a second thought. To do so is to disrespect roughly three thousand years of history and scholarship. The readings discussed here are presented as a fresh or alternative interpretation to hold in conjunction with or alongside more traditional ones. Our faith can be a "yes, and . . ." faith: "Yes, I understand that particular interpretation of Scripture, and I also see how this other reading is consistent with truth as well and could also be valid." We are mature enough that we do not have to be beholden to black-and-white thinking. We can hold our old ideas and new ones together simultaneously. We can compare, contrast, stack, blend, and layer meaning even as we contend with the harder side of belief—the feelings like anger, apathy, or abandonment.

I am not a psychologist, nor do I claim to be. I have a doctorate in literature with some theological training mixed in; my business is words—specifically, the impact of words on attitudes, identity, culture, and the way we create meaning. My primary concern in this book is how the sacred words of Scripture have been used to shame, alienate, manipulate, and control. Language has power, and it does not take a psychologist to see how the misapplication of this power, whether intentional or not, has led to unhealthy dynamics within many churches and church traditions.

In no way does this study imply that the Bible doesn't matter, or that it should be discounted as unimportant or pushed aside as irrelevant; on the contrary. The Bible is our introduction to God. It is how we learn the framework of our faith and the history of humanity's engagement with the Almighty. It shows us what faith and trust look like by introducing us to the ancient patriarchs and matriarchs who paved the way. The Bible is how we learn how to recognize God in our world, how we find hope in struggle, and how we share that hope with those around us. The Bible is what prepares us to face life armed with the knowledge that will form the foundation of spiritual maturity. The Bible is the beginning, but not the end, of how we come to know God.

Our ultimate aim as believers should not be to follow the Bible as literally as possible—modern writers like A. J. Jacobs and Rachel Held Evans already proved the futility of such efforts[4]—but to take from it what we can to make sense of a world full of unexpected and unpredictable circumstances. It is the difference between being taught *what* to think and being taught *how* to think. The Bible exists to give us a foundation with which we can approach life and interact with the world, not a list of catchy phrases that we can attach willy-nilly to any situation and declare them binding promises. Unfortunately, this is often how Scripture is treated—as God's absolute verdict for every possible scenario. If your situation does not reflect the accepted meaning of the verse or story, something must be wrong with *you*.

The Bible is the beginning, but not the end, of how we come to know God.

When we try to shoehorn Scriptures into every situation—even ones where they are not applicable—*we deny what the Holy Spirit is telling us at that moment* in favor of passages written in a specific time and place to a specific group of people living a specific set of circumstances. In doing so, we make a mockery of those God-breathed words and an idol out of ideologies. Scripture was intended to give us a framework so we could confidently interact with the world as we employ our God-given intellect, emotions, and reason—not ignore them.[5] Why else would God have given us the Holy Spirit as a comforter and guide if God did not want us to pay attention to and draw truth from our world here and now, as we are living in it? As Jesus tells his followers in John 14:26: "But the Advocate, the Holy Spirit, whom the Father will send in my name, will teach you everything, and remind you of all that I have said to you." It is a two-part job: teaching, which implies learning new things, *and* reminding the believer of Jesus's words. Discovering new ways of understanding God *and* recalling Scripture. Lived experienced *and* traditional religious lessons. The role of the Holy Spirit is literally to show us how to marry the two.

That is at the heart of what I hope you will find in the coming pages: a reconciliation between the things you know from experience to be true and the questions or feelings you may have been told were sinful, wrong, or invalid. Facts are provable, concrete, and undeniable, whereas God is a force and presence we accept on faith alone. Therefore, if the facts as we know them fail to fit God, then perhaps we need to change our understanding of God to make sense of the facts. We seek not to remake the Lord in our own image but to expand our understanding of an infinitely complex Almighty by opening our eyes to other facets we have ignored, explained away, or never even imagined could exist.

o o o

On June 21, 2001, Britain dedicated a memorial in honor of the soldiers who were executed for cowardice or desertion in World War I. Named *Shot at Dawn*, the statue pays tribute to the approximately twenty thousand men who were judged guilty of offenses that warranted the death penalty. Three thousand were handed sentences of execution, and 346 of those execution orders actually took place. The statue itself, a blindfolded man tied to a stake as he awaits the firing squad, was modeled after Private Herbert Burden, who lied about his age to enlist in the army to fight for king and country. Burden was executed on July 21, 1915, at age seventeen. Around the statue are stakes bearing the names of all the soldiers from the war who also suffered Burden's fate. The memorial bears witness to the carnage committed by a group of old men in power whose outdated understanding of trauma and the conditions of modern warfare condemned scared and suffering humans to death—leaders who placed ideals and axioms over basic humanity.

Perhaps, in time, our churches will make a similar gesture of regret and contrition for the abuses heaped upon struggling souls. But until that happens, we must plead our own defense and fight for our own survival in the conflict to which we have pledged our lives and souls. When we feel alienated, condemned, or otherwise shamed for an unorthodox path to faith or spiritual fatigue that is not cured with a quick sermon and easy, one-size-fits-all advice, we must take it upon ourselves to follow the charge of Philippians 2:12–13: "Work out your own salvation with fear and trembling; for it is God who is at work in you."

2

ASKING:
THE GOD WHO DEMANDS TOO MUCH

Exodus 5
Job 13
Luke 18

In the summer of 1951, my grandfather was a nineteen-year-old salesman at a shoe store in Sheboygan, Wisconsin. Smart, hardworking, and friendly, he enjoyed his job and already had his eye on the managerial track, but he found himself facing a question from customers and even the occasional meddling stranger: "Why is an able-bodied young man like you selling shoes instead of serving in Korea?"

Always the same question, always the same slight note of derision. Each time, he looked the person in the eye and replied, "Well, I'm a 5A."

The questioner would raise an eyebrow, purse their lips, and say, "You mean 5F? You failed the physical?"

"No," Grandpa replied. "5A. I'm the sole surviving son."

The challenge was instantly dropped.

5A status, which later became codified as Department of Defense directive 1315.15 (also known as the "Sole Surviving Son Policy"), meant that a young man who had already lost a sibling in combat and was the family's only remaining son was exempt from the draft. In my grandfather's case, his brother, Able Baker Donald Yecke, US Navy, had died two weeks shy of his twenty-first birthday, in April 1945, during the Battle of Okinawa, when a kamikaze pilot struck his ship, the USS *Emmons*. Donald was buried at sea.

Directive 1315.15 became law in 1948, following numerous stories of families losing multiple children in military service during World War II. What the nation realized was that, at some point, the ask becomes too great a burden for one family to bear.

Unfortunately, there is no 5A status or directive 1315.15 for the Christian walk. There is no legal protection, no bridge too far when the scope or depth of sacrifices God asks of us begins to offend our sense of proportion. There is no point at which we are permitted to say, "I have given you everything you have asked; this is now too much. I am done." Just the opposite, in fact. We praise people who have made extreme sacrifices of life and limb for the gospel; we call them "saints" and hold them up as the example of radical faith to which we should all strive. We look at people who have had everything stripped from them due to disease or disaster, we see families that have endured multiple traumas, we shake our heads at the string of heartbreaks that seem to plague certain lives, and we ask the age-old question, "Why do bad things happen to good people?" We lift them up in prayer, send them reassuring Scriptures, encourage them to stay strong, and silently (maybe even guiltily) thank God it isn't us.

Until it is.

Suddenly, the unthinkable becomes reality. The kind of tragedy that only happens to other people suddenly hits us. The burdens we once were grateful we didn't have to carry now land squarely on our shoulders, and no Scripture, no prayer, no word of encouragement seems to make the load any lighter. Maybe we recite Matthew 11:30, "For my yoke is easy, and my burden is light," and it feels like a lie. Almost inevitably, someone repeats perhaps the worst cliché in the English language: "God won't give you more than you can bear," and we *know* it is a lie because our reality, right here and right now, is already much greater than we can possibly stand.

And yet, so often it feels like there are people watching us in the church, and if we raise our voice to question, if we dare to challenge God's mercy, if we shake our fist at the heavens and demand to know why, they tell us we are out of line. Such faith tantrums are the purview of petulant children, not mature believers, they reason. Maybe someone quotes Isaiah 55:8–9 at us:

> For my thoughts are not your thoughts,
>> nor are your ways my ways, says the LORD.
> For as the heavens are higher than the earth,
>> so are my ways higher than your ways,
>> and my thoughts than your thoughts.

And they act as though this verse somehow erases all injustice, indignity, and suffering. Or perhaps we are told to remember Romans 8:28, "We know that all things work together for good for those who love God, who are called according to his purpose"—as if we just need to play the long game instead of questioning whether the resulting good is even worth it. Or we might be prodded with James 1:2-3, "My brothers and sisters, whenever you face trials of any kind, consider it nothing but joy, because you know that the testing of your faith produces endurance"—which implies that a lack of happiness or gratefulness in the face of soul-crushing pain somehow signals a superficial faith.

In short, we are told that whatever we are *experiencing* is incorrect, insufficient, or inaccurate, and we would be better served to deny it, push it down, or recast it as a cause for praise. Rather than acknowledging the reality and validity of our feelings, we are taught to alter our truth so that it falls into line with words written thousands of years ago by specific people to address specific situations that are wholly unique from our current circumstances. It's almost as if we've been told, "If you can't say something nice about God, don't say anything at all."

° ° °

Heather is one of three siblings in a tight-knit midwestern family.¹ As we sit inside on a cold afternoon in early February, the ground is covered in a fresh blanket of snow, temporarily smoothing over the jagged lines of frozen mud underneath; it seems an apt setting for the calm veneer Heather was expected to put on her emotional turmoil. She describes to me how, in high school, her older sibling was diagnosed with a terminal illness. Three years later, Heather's younger sibling was critically injured in an accident. The children were all active in the church youth group growing up, and their parents' main social life was with the other members of their congregation. But all that church time couldn't prepare Heather for everything life threw her way. The repeated traumas her family experienced were bad enough, but just as bad was the "good face" she was told to put on the whole situation:

> For a long time it felt like we just couldn't catch a break as a family. The awful stuff just kept happening and there wasn't any sort of explanation or reason for it—it was just like we couldn't catch our breath. A lot of people were supportive, but I still heard people basically saying, "You shouldn't question God. He has his reasons for all of this." That just seemed wrong to me. God demanded so much from our family, but we weren't supposed to question it? We were just supposed to accept it with a smile and no argument? I mean, if that's the case, that's not a God I want any part of. It was awful to watch my siblings go through all of that and watch my parents suffer along with them as they tried to hold it all together. It's too much for one family. I should be allowed to feel that way. My faith should be big enough for me to be able to look at all the awful things we went through in such a short time and say, "That's not fair." Because it's not. And if God is love, then he should feel the same way. And if he doesn't, then what kind of God is that?

The kind of denial or dismissal of genuine emotion that Heather describes can drive people out of churches because it isn't just insensitive, it's dishonest. What's more, *it's not even biblical*. Scripture is littered with examples of prophets, patriarchs, and regular people openly expressing their discontent or refusing to rejoice in the lot that has befallen them.

Consider Elijah in 1 Kings 19, who, after fleeing into the wilderness pursued by Jezebel's wrath, throws himself under a tree and begs God to let him die: "It is enough; now, O LORD, take away my life, for I am no better than my ancestors" (19:4). He falls into a deep sleep, is awakened by an angel, who brings him warm bread and a jug of water, and then falls asleep again. After this, we are told: "The angel of the LORD came a second time, touched him, and said, 'Get up and eat, otherwise the journey will be too much for you.' He got up, and ate and drank; then he went in the strength of that food forty days and forty nights to Horeb the mount of God" (19:7–8). It's not just that Elijah, one of God's most stalwart prophets, was pushed past his breaking point; as more than one friend has told me, their mother loved to point to this story as illustrating the tremendous power of a nap and a snack. That's not merely a punch line of weary parents trying to help a cranky child; it's a very valid point. Sometimes—oftentimes— this kind of basic renewal and revival is exactly what we need to power forward through awful circumstances.

In Genesis 21, we see Hagar and Ishmael cast out of Abraham's camp and banished to the wilderness. When mother and son are out of water and on the verge of death, Hagar places the boy under some bushes and steps away, saying to God, "Do not let me see the boy die." After she cries out to God in utter despair, the Lord answers with assurances that her son will father a nation. "Then God opened her eyes and she saw a well of water. She went, and filled the skin with water, and gave the boy a drink" (21:19). Whether by divine intervention or simply self-care, attending to our physical needs can help our emotional state tremendously.

But, of course, this is hardly helpful advice in the face of a devastating diagnosis or bankruptcy or a house fire or divorce or a global pandemic. Sometimes, we are beset by deep and soul-crushing burdens that won't look better after a good night's sleep or a decent meal. Some hurts are too significant to look better in the morning. And that's when we turn to Job—good old, long-suffering, broken-hearted, sore-covered, lecture-enduring, sackcloth-and-ashes-wearing Job.

One of the Scriptures most commonly quoted both to and by Christians struggling with unfathomable suffering is Job 13:15, where Job declares:

> "Though He slay me,
> I will hope in Him." (NASB)

The message of unshakable, even desperate faith and trust in the Lord is clear. We cling tightly to God even when we do not understand, and we do so humbly, submitting ourselves to God's will. This verse is a profound pronouncement of radical submission: "It doesn't matter what God does to me; I will remain faithful." The statement paints Job's relationship to God as unwavering and unhesitating, with no reservations and zero pushback. We might even be tempted to regard it as one of slavish devotion. Pause for a moment to consider how this verse strikes you: Does it fill you with admiration or make you deeply uncomfortable? After all, what some may interpret as a beautiful portrait of faith, others view as an endorsement of abuse. Do you regard Job's unquestioning commitment as admirable or dangerous? Either reading is valid, but if you've only been taught to interpret it one way, it can be a challenge to sit with the emotions on the other side of it, especially if they feel problematic or even sacrilegious.

Note, however, that the passage cited above is not the whole verse; there is a second half of Job 13:15 that is often ignored. The Scripture in its entirety reads:

> "Though He slay me,
> I will hope in Him.
> *Nevertheless I will argue my ways before Him.*" (NASB)

Other translations phrase it:

> "Though he slay me, yet I will hope in him;
>   I will surely defend my ways to his face" (NIV)

and

> "See, he will kill me; I have no hope;
>   but I will defend my ways to his face." (NRSV)

Suddenly, the ultimate verse on submission seems a whole lot less submissive.

Reading the first part in isolation, we see Job affirming the unquestioning acceptance of his lot. But when the second sentence is juxtaposed with the first, the passage conveys a very different meaning; the latter half challenges any passivity implied in the first. The Hebrew word that begins the second sentence is often translated alternately as "nevertheless," "surely," or "however." It indicates a contrast to what came before—not a negation, but a turn on whatever the earlier sentiment was: "X may be true; *even so,* Y is also true." In Job's case, it communicates: "Though God injures me, I will hold tight to him. *But still,* I will argue my case to his face."

Equally significant is the Hebrew word that translates "face" or "countenance." Job does not want to grovel at the hem of God's garment; he is demanding a full audience with the Almighty. He is daring to confront God face-to-face—the same face that Moses begged to see and from whom Isaiah noted the cherubim averted their eyes in holy reverence. This is not a trembling, apologetic petition; this is a statement of defiance and righteous anger—a full-blown interrogation. In fact, the

opening verse of Job's rebuttal to his friends makes clear his
stance on the matter:

> "But I would speak to the Almighty,
>   And I desire to argue with God." (13:3 NASB)

Job is shameless in his terms of engagement, and he does not
stop there. Not only does he unflinchingly demand his audience
with God but in verse 16 he says this confrontation "will be my
salvation, / For a godless man may not come before His presence"
(NASB). Job's argument is not simply a tantrum tolerated by God;
it is the very source of his salvation. The mere fact that he has the
ability to question the Almighty means that he is morally worthy
of such an exchange. Forget any self-flagellating or "for such a
worm as I" talk (no offense to Isaac Watts); Job does not view
himself as a wretched creature odious to God but as a faithful (if
fallible) creation from the hand of the Most High. Job recognizes
that his upright intentions and moral actions mean he has a right
to ponder such questions. God may not answer them, but neither
does God strike Job down for asking. Job knows that the burden
he has been given to shoulder is more than a just God should logi-
cally allow. Only because he has striven to live morally and understand what he can about the Almighty is Job able to recognize the
apparent disconnect between what is fair and what is excessive.
Job has not abandoned his belief when he questions God; if anything, his faith is stronger than ever. When Job seeks to hold God
accountable for the suffering he has endured, he is affirming his
belief in the benevolent nature of God and the divine promises
by pointing out apparent inconsistencies. Job has not turned his
back on God; he's just recalibrating his understanding of who God
is and how the cosmic order works.

But the book of Job is an exceptional case. By some accounts,
it is a rare glimpse behind the divine curtain into the heavenly
realms; by other accounts, it is a divinely inspired fable that il-

lustrates the complexities of suffering. For a more concrete look at God-condoned arguing, let us consider another example that is central to the founding history of the Israelite nation and the establishment and codification of Jewish religious law.

In Exodus 5, we read about Moses's request that the enslaved Israelites be allowed to go to the desert to worship. When Pharaoh answers with charges of laziness and demands that they now find their own straw while also increasing the quota for bricks, the distress in Moses's voice is obvious. He confronts God, asking: "O Lord, why have you mistreated this people? Why did you ever send me? Since I first came to Pharaoh to speak in your name, he has mistreated this people, and you have done nothing at all to deliver your people" (5:22-23).

This is not a humble, groveling request. Moses is not meekly asking God for guidance on the difficult road ahead. Consider the bold charges Moses lays before God in his prayer:

1. You, God, have been an instrument of harm toward your people.
2. You should never have asked me to speak to Pharaoh.
3. Things have only gotten worse since I have invoked your name.
4. You have not lifted a finger to help us.

Rather than accepting the situation as it is by simply acknowledging that God is in control, Moses pushes back. He knows that the situation is untenable. He knows that the burden placed on the people is excessive and unmerited. He knows that God is asking more of him than he feels capable of offering. And he does not take this lying down.

Throughout the biblical narrative we see example after example of people challenging God when the burden of sacred demands seems unfair instead of dutifully accepting their lot without a fight or even extending their bowls like Oliver Twist and begging, "Please, sir, I want some more." Cain tells God, "My punishment is greater than I can bear!" (Gen. 4:13). Even Jesus

begs God, saying, "Let this cup pass from me," before his crucifixion (Matt. 26:39). One of the most consistent traits of biblical
figures is that they challenge God, sometimes even directly. And
yet many of our modern churches have somehow deemed this
action shameful or even sinful.

Largely missing from modern Christian theology is the notion
that we have any place to question God or the Scriptures, but this
blind allegiance would have been foreign to Jesus, whose entire
religious upbringing was defined by debates about Jewish law
conducted between religious teachers. In fact, Judaism actively
encourages debate with God; this is the basis for the Talmud and
Midrash, which record two thousand years of written dialogue
with the Holy Scriptures. These texts are second only to the Scriptures themselves in Judaism. In fact, this kind of holy argumen-
tation is considered a moral imperative within the Jewish faith,
dating back at least to the seventh century BCE, when God commands the Jews to form courts to debate matters of religious law
in Deuteronomy 16:18. Many scholars maintain that the tradition
goes back even further, to when Moses appointed leaders who
"judged the people at all times; hard cases they brought to Moses,
but any minor case they decided themselves" (Exod. 18:26).

Each court, or "house of judgment," was the official seat of the
"matters of litigation" of the holy text, but it was not the only place
such dialogue could occur. In fact, debate with the text is one of the
corner pieces of Jewish culture, and Jesus himself engaged in such
intellectual exercises. Throughout the Sermon on the Mount, for
example, Jesus repeats "You have heard it said . . . but I tell you . . ."
In this manner, he is challenging the traditional interpretation of
the text supplied by the religious leaders, encouraging his followers instead to consider that the text might mean something very
different from what they have been taught to believe.

When we break down the means by which our genuine dialogue with God is recast as shameful or sacrilegious ("I'm
surprised you would question him; I thought your faith was

stronger than that!" or "Who are you to be mad at God? God saved you from hell"), we begin to see how deeply engrained certain power structures are in our theology. Despite the fact that such challenges are absolutely modeled for us throughout the scriptural text, somewhere along the way many of us were taught not to question God, ecclesiastical authority, or the Scriptures as they are taught to us. Such thinking has changed faith from a *process* or a *conversation* by which we engage with God to a static, unmoving, one-sided *state of being*—something that simply is or is not. We have reduced faith from something we *do* to something we merely possess, couching it in the binary terms of "having" and "losing" instead of seeing it for what it really is: a living, dynamic series of exchanges that cause it to expand and contract with the natural rhythms of life. In fact, in the opening passages of Isaiah, God even invites Judah to engage in such a dialogue:

> Come now, let us argue it out,
>   says the LORD. (1:18)

Ours is a God who welcomes engagement; God does not want mindless automatons who fail to question, challenge, or fight. Too often we focus on the meek inheriting the earth while ignoring the fact that Jesus included zealots in his handpicked group of disciples. God has a place for people of strength, determination, and courage—people with a little pluck. God is okay with pushback. This is, after all, the same God who bargained with Abraham, who wrestled with Jacob, and who listened to Jesus's desperate prayers as he begged to be spared the brutal humiliation and execution to come.

Holocaust survivor and Nobel Peace Prize recipient Elie Wiesel spoke about an event he observed while a prisoner in Auschwitz in 1944, when three devout rabbis decided to charge God with the crime of permitting the slaughter of the Jewish people. This experience stayed with Wiesel for the rest of his life, eventually inspiring his play *The Trial of God*, which he published in 1979. Using a story-within-a-story format in the play, Wiesel describes three rabbis in seventeenth-century Ukraine who hold a mock "house of judgment" in which they argue whether or not God is just or fair following a pogrom that has wiped out all but two Jews of a village. As someone who survived unimaginable horrors, Wiesel placed the problem of human suffering at the heart of his writing. How are humans to relate to a God who seems to violate God's own laws? How do we shoulder a load too great to carry? And what place does faith have in a life that has been (or is actively being) shaped by trauma?

Psychologists break trauma down into three main types: acute, chronic, and complex. **Acute** trauma is a onetime painful or dangerous event such as a terrible accident or a deep personal loss. **Chronic** trauma is ongoing, long-term exposure to highly distressing situations like combat or abuse. **Complex** trauma occurs when multiple unrelated or loosely affiliated traumas converge—for example, a dire medical diagnosis on the heels of job loss or the death of a child leading to the collapse of a marriage. There is even a kind of auxiliary category for **vicarious** trauma, where people close to the victim manifest signs of trauma due to their emotional proximity to the situation.

But whatever the type of trauma, grief is rarely straightforward; the result is often a jumble of multiple emotional injuries that form a complicated web of mourning. A home invasion leaves the victim feeling violated and anxious even though the danger is past. A worldwide pandemic can lead to depression, fear, job loss, eviction, and political instability. Medical malpractice is not limited to the botched procedure itself but possibly involves lies, cover-ups, and blame-shifting to avoid a lawsuit. Sexual assault is often not only about the horrific violence itself but also about the victim shaming that may follow. (*What was she wearing? Was she drinking? Why was she at that party in the first place?*) Add to these complexities factors like post-traumatic stress disorder, trauma bonds, mental health challenges, regret, second guessing, survivor's guilt—and the whole matter becomes infinitely more complicated. And as these complications mount, the already too-heavy burden becomes increasingly impossible to shoulder. Trauma rarely occurs in isolation; it is simply the catalyst of ongoing grief that can magnify or trigger other issues as it accumulates.

The easy response, of course, is to say that we were never meant to shoulder these kinds of afflictions alone; the church exists, in large part, to help us bear the loads. Our brothers and sisters are meant to come alongside us, sharing the weight and holding us up when we feel our knees begin to buckle. We recognize the beauty of Aaron and Hur faithfully holding up Moses's arms against the Amalekites when Moses becomes too exhausted to lift them himself (Exod. 17:12–14). We "bear one another's burdens, and thereby fulfill the law of Christ" (Gal. 6:2 NASB). But where many suffering, struggling believers face an additional challenge is in the tension between acceptable and unacceptable grief—namely, the things it is socially okay to mourn publicly and the things that propriety asks us to keep under wraps. Sometimes, the ask is just too great, and there are burdens that the church simply cannot bear for one another.

For example, it is socially acceptable to mourn the loss of a job, but the loss of a pregnancy is often something that makes people uncomfortable to dwell on. We can publicly fret about declining health but give the side-eye to someone bringing up a crumbling marriage. We ask for prayers to combat our problem with worry but usually not for our problem with anger.

If we have to give our grief a name in the public eye, we often choose only the most palatable façade we can give it. As a result, our "acceptable grief" ends up shouldering the burden for all the trauma it's *not* acceptable to talk about. What is passed off as never-ending professional demands may actually be the mask a person places over the stress of a spouse with an addiction. Ex-

cessive public worry over a child's report card could be the con-
duit for the heartbreak of infidelity. Prolonged angst over a seemingly minor car accident may also carry the fear and anxiety of
ongoing infertility. To outsiders, the responses may seem out-
sized or the coping mechanisms might look like overreactions as
we channel all our private suffering into the one outlet it is okay
to share. We present socially acceptable challenges as a cover
story for our much deeper grief, even as the accumulating pain
compounds and cuts even deeper. Grief often carries the weight
of every trauma—the ones we share as well as the things we cannot say. And this may include mourning a loss of faith, disappointment in the church, or disillusionment with a God who
would allow so much heartache.

This is not intended to put the onus of sharing on the suffering
individual; it is a deeply personal choice regarding what to make
public and what to keep private. Every person has reasons and
boundaries. No one should feel shamed into sharing more than is
right for them; however, we should feel free to suffer *un*-silently
before God—even (especially) with the burdens we must carry
alone. If something seems excessive, tell God. Give voice to not only
your troubles but also your troubles *about* your troubles. You do
not have to accept your pain gratefully or
even quietly. You are not failing if you fail
to rejoice in your current circumstances,
nor are you angering God if you feel anger toward him. It's okay to protest your
innocence before God, just as Job did. You
are allowed to experience your God-given
emotions. Disagreement, disappointment, or dissatisfaction with
the Divine does not make a blasphemer out of a believer. The honest expression of heartbreak signals trust in God far more than any
inauthentic response dressed up in flowery Scriptures.

*Grief often carries the
weight of every trauma—
the ones we share as well as
the things we cannot say.*

Luke 18 contains a collection of stories with a similar theme:
genuine responses to God. Jesus moves swiftly from the parable

of the persistent widow, who challenges the judge over and over until he rules in her favor, to the story of the Pharisee and the publican wherein a sinful, broken man's honest prayers are valued above the disingenuous words of someone wrapped in religious trappings. Jesus then moves away from parables when he rebukes those who would try to keep children from pestering him, "for it is to such as these that the kingdom of God belongs" (18:16). Next, he speaks with the "rich young ruler" who believed the key to eternal life required more than he felt able to give; when asked if *anyone* could possibly be saved by such righteous standards, Jesus replies, "What is impossible for mortals is possible for God" (18:23, 27). Rather than condemning the young man for his honest reaction, Jesus offers hope. Finally, we meet a man who is blind, who cries out loudly to Jesus to give him sight. The leaders of the crowd tried to shame the man; they "sternly ordered him to be quiet; but he shouted even more loudly" (18:39). One after another, these stories present a common theme: we can and should approach God openly, honestly, and free of pretense. Christ welcomes these engagements—these pushy, uncouth, messy, disillusioned, disruptive, *genuine* engagements—just as much, if not more, than the polite, tidy, acceptable ones.

You are allowed to experience your God-given emotions.

It is true, of course, that the people in Luke 18 had the luxury of seeing Jesus face-to-face; for us, approaching God may feel at times like nothing more than screaming into the proverbial void. That might be the hardest part of all of this to reconcile: God may ask too much of us without ever offering an explanation. We are not promised answers, but we are granted the freedom to question.

Asked toward the end of his life how the religious trial he witnessed in Auschwitz turned out, Wiesel replied: "At the end of the trial, they used the word *chayav*, rather than 'guilty.' It means 'He owes us something.' Then we went to pray."[2]

They tried God. They found God wanting. They worshiped God anyway.

Because that is what faith is—not the certainty of answers but the active process of engaging with your beliefs in real and authentic ways. It is the hope that God exists beyond the questions, beyond the doubt, beyond the pain. It is the assurance that when we seek God there—in that uncharted space that lies beyond certainty instead of in the stained-glass platitudes of unwavering devotion—God will be waiting to receive us.

3

APATHY:
THE GOD WHO DOESN'T SEEM TO CARE

Luke 10:38–42
Mark 4:35–41

"**M**ake sure you ask for another ultrasound. A friend of mine was told her baby had died, but we all surrounded that family and prayed. And when she went in for the operation to remove it, it turned out that the heart was beating away, strong as can be. It just goes to show the power of faith and prayer. Remember 1 Peter 5:7: 'Cast all your anxiety upon him, because he cares for you.'"

These were the words a dear friend and pastor offered to me in October 2009, when my husband was deployed in Afghanistan and the long-awaited pregnancy that had finally tested positive just five days after he shipped out in July now showed no signs of life at sixteen weeks. My surgery was scheduled for four days out, and there was no shortage of praying, along with weeping, begging, fasting, shouting at the heavens, and any other possible way of petitioning God. Surely with a husband on the other side of the globe in a combat zone and my family a thousand miles away, God wouldn't abandon me now. If ever there was a time for a miracle, this was it.

Yet when October 30 came and I was rolled into the operating room with my arms still wrapped desperately around my belly, there was no surprise cancellation. My faith and my prayers were, apparently, not powerful enough to stir sudden signs of life.

My friend sent flowers. God stayed silent.

◦ ◦ ◦

Our world can turn upside down when it seems we care more than God does. According to the old adage, "There is no such thing as unanswered prayers; there is just 'yes,' 'no,' and 'not right now.'" But for anyone who has ever petitioned God through tears and brokenness and heard only crickets in return, this is hardly reassuring. Jesus tells his disciples in Luke 11: "Is there anyone among you who, if your child asks for a fish, will give a snake instead of a fish? Or if the child asks for an egg, will give a scorpion? If you then, who are evil, know how to give good gifts to your children, how much more will the heavenly Father give the Holy Spirit to those who ask him!" (11:11-14). Yet how many of us have ever reached a point where we would be content with a snake or a scorpion for no other reason than it proved God was at least acknowledging our prayers rather than relegating them to a celestial junk mail file?

Often it seems we can only spot God's work in retrospect, as if all the evidence contrary to divine indifference is only at the ending of the story. It is there that we can finally see proof that God did indeed act. The challenge, of course, is that we don't know the ending of our story when we are in the middle of it. We can't jump ahead to the moral takeaways the way we can skip ahead in the Bible when we already know the outcome and see what was going on behind the scenes all along. When we are waiting for our own deliverance, the lack of resolution (or even just improvement) can feel as if God simply doesn't care—especially when Scripture, sermon illustrations, and other people's situations around us are full of signs of divine intervention. What do we do when it seems as if God is indifferent to our suffering, and all we can see is what is in front of us rather than the greater good we have been taught to believe God is always crafting in the background?

Perhaps the best answer to this question comes from examining what happens when someone poses it directly, as Martha of Bethany does in Luke 10. The consummate hostess, Martha bustles about the house "distracted by her many tasks" while her sister Mary sits at Jesus's feet. In frustration, Martha finally blurts out, "Lord, do you not care that my sister has left me to do all the work by myself?" She is then gently corrected by Jesus, who reminds her that Mary has made the better choice.

This story is usually presented as a rebuke for getting so caught up in the hustle and bustle of life that we forget the beauty of simply sitting and listening to God, but it also gives us a more far-reaching lesson, namely, how we should respond when we feel so overlooked or unappreciated that we must call God's attention to our plight.

A closer look at the language of the story reveals some interesting details that may further elucidate the nuances of this exchange. First, the Greek word used here to indicate Martha's "tasks" (*diakonia*) is often translated "ministry," "service," "preparation," or "providing relief." In fact, this story is the only time in most translations of the New Testament that this term is rendered "tasks." Often, readers make the assumption that Martha's work entails domestic duties tied to hosting Jesus, but the text never actually states that. All it says is that she was "distracted by much ministry." This choice of words is significant because it doesn't automatically imply that Martha was annoyed because Mary wasn't helping her carry out basic chores like sweeping or washing dishes; these are assumptions we read into the text culturally, but they may not reflect reality. Another Greek word (*ergon*) actually appears 174 times in the New Testament to indicate work in the sense of "deeds" or "tasks." Earlier in the same chapter as Martha and Mary's story, Luke even uses a related word (*ergamai*; 11:2) for workmen or laborers in the field who gather the harvest. The distinction seems deliberate; the things that occupy Martha are not just the tedious chores of daily life; they are weighty, significant works requiring specialized skills. The point is that Martha's labors, whatever they were—possibly tied to hospitality and caring for the domestic sphere but possibly not—were a ministry. This is not meaningless busywork that pulled her focus, as is often implied. And it is here that God's seeming apathy can sometimes sting the most: when it seems God takes little interest in the work we are trying to do on behalf of the kingdom.

There may be inherent sexism in the traditional translations that relegate Martha's work to mere chores or tasks rather than considering it a full-fledged ministry or skilled service, as the word is translated everywhere else when applied to men or to mixed-gender groups. This is a historic problem that continues in many churches today, when God is imagined to place higher inherent value on the work of preachers or leaders, who are traditionally men, than on those whose ministries are not out in front, as is often the case with ministries conducted by women in many complementarian churches. In these situations, people are sometimes taught by example, if not by words, that God does not care as much about their "tasks" as about those in "serious ministry." If we take nothing else from the story of Martha and Mary, let it be that Jesus *always* cared more about the person than the work, as we will see.

What does Jesus tell Martha *actually* matters? Depending on the translation, he says something along the lines of "You are distracted by many things, but only one thing matters." The word rendered "but" (or sometimes "however," or sometimes just left untranslated) is the Greek conjunction *de*, which is a surprisingly versatile word. It can be used as a negation, as it is traditionally translated here, but it can also function in two other ways. First, it can serve simply as a verbal clue that the sentence is continuing (in which case it may be rendered as "now" or simply denoted through the use of punctuation like a semicolon). Secondly, *de* can be translated as "and." This minuscule wording change might influence the impact of Jesus's remark:

"You are distracted by many things, *but* only one thing matters . . ."

versus

"You are distracted by many things, *and* only one thing matters . . ."

While the distinction is incredibly minor, it is real. The use of the word "but" in the top sentence negates the first half of the passage so that the implication is: "There are many things, but only one matters." The use of the word "and" in the second sentence, however, incorporates the "one thing" into the many that Martha is undertaking, implying: "You are doing many things, and one of them is the thing that matters most." In the first sentence, Martha has neglected or overlooked worship; in the second one, Martha has deprioritized it, but it is not altogether separate from the actions of her ministry. The first reading is a correction; the second is a reminder. Neither is a condemnation.

Even more significantly, Martha's primary frustration stems not from the fact that Mary isn't helping with chores but from the fact that Jesus has failed to acknowledge Martha's effort. Remember that her initial statement is directed at Jesus's failure to act, not Mary's: "Lord, do you not care [literally 'does it not concern you'] that my sister has left me to do all the work by myself?" Martha's first concern is not that she has to shoulder the responsibility alone, but that Jesus doesn't even seem to notice. Mary's disengagement is the basis for the provoking situation, but the thing that finally makes Martha throw up her hands in exasperation is Jesus's apparent indifference.

Jesus's reply reveals so much not only in the obvious sense, where he honors Mary's choice to worship, but also on a deeper level, demonstrating how God receives and reacts to an honest outburst at his disappointing response. Jesus does not admonish Martha as he does the Pharisees; he doesn't thunder, "Woe to you for rebuking the Son of God!" or even "Woman, check your tone." Instead, he replies graciously, repeating her name gently and pointing out her worried and distracted behavior, but not shaming her for it; he simply emphasizes the wisdom of Mary's choice. Jesus does not reprimand Martha for expressing her frustration or even for directing it toward him; he actually comforts her in the midst of her anxiety. This is further supported by the different verbs that are often both translated "distracted." The first, which describes the impact Martha's ministry is having on her attention to Jesus, is *perispaō*, which literally means "to draw away" (10:40); this is the only use of the word in the entire New Testament. The second instance of the word "distracted" in this story comes in the following verse, when Jesus points out to Martha that she is *merimnaō* and *thorybazō*, usually translated "worried and distracted" by many things. Interestingly, however, the literal translation is more like "anxious and troubled"; the second word means "to be upset/agitated." In other words, Jesus is every bit as concerned with the emotional turmoil Martha is experiencing as he is with her distracted attention.

There are several takeaways from this passage. The most apparent one, of course, is that kingdom-serving ministries, not just the busyness of life, can sometimes pull us away from Jesus when we lose sight of whom we are serving. But just as much, this story is about being in the moment and feeling what we are feeling—as Martha and Mary both do—rather than trying to crowd everything else out with our individual missions. *"Lord, don't you care?"* God does, which is why, instead of focusing on the public face of how we encounter the Almighty, we should instead focus on authentic engagement—which includes the honest expression of our emotions.

The truth is, we often imagine every biblical figure interacting with God the way Isaiah did. When he is asked to undertake a commission too great for his ability, he allows God to purify his lips with a burning coal and offers the oft-quoted Scripture of enthusiastic evangelists: "Here am I, Lord. Send me!" Isaiah yields completely to God without question or complaint. But the exchange between Martha and Jesus is significant because it shows us the legitimacy and importance of acknowledging our emotions—feeling them exactly as they are, and exactly as we are, in the moment—even when God's actions in that same moment don't necessarily make sense to us. Mary, of course, also illustrates this same point: she chooses to sit in the moment and feel whatever awe and wonder she is experiencing at Jesus's feet, and he praises her for it. These examples force us to slow down and feel our feelings instead of trying to explain them away or ignore them altogether. They show us that we can interact with God in a truthful way, finding significance in what might be revealed to us in our authentic emotions instead of rushing ahead to the end, as if that were the only part of the story that matters.

This same theme is present in Mark 4, where we find an exhausted Jesus asleep on some pillows in the stern of a boat as he and his followers cross the Sea of Galilee in a small fleet. When a storm blows up that threatens to sink their vessels, the other passengers wake him and cry, "Teacher, do you not care that we are perishing?" (4:38). Jesus's response is twofold: "He woke up and rebuked the wind, and said to the sea, 'Peace! Be still!' Then the wind ceased, and there was a dead calm. He said to them, 'Why are you afraid? Have you still no faith?'" (4:39-40).

Once again, when Jesus is presented with the exact same question Martha asks of him in Luke 10—"Don't you care?" (it's even the exact same phrasing in the Greek)—we see the honest expression of emotions that results in correction but not condemnation.

The first thing Jesus does upon waking is not to reproach his followers but to "rebuke" the wind; the verb used is *epitimaō*, which means "to censure" or "to warn." When he turns to the scared passengers in the boat, however, Jesus does not also rebuke them; rather, he merely replies to them; the text uses a simple verb of speech (*legō*), meaning "he answered" or "he said." Jesus's response challenges them, but it does not chastise them; the differentiation in Mark's word choice makes that clear. Jesus scolds the wind, but he does not scold the questioner for asking.

How frustrating and even terrifying it can be when it feels like we have to rouse God to get some attention—when we find ourselves crying out, "Wake up! Can't you see what's going on? Don't you care that I need you?" We are told in Matthew 6:8 that God knows our needs before we even ask, and yet it can be hard to interpret silence to our most heartfelt pleas as anything other than a lack of concern. The thing is, God is anything but indifferent. When we read how God's wrath "burned against" various people or about the assorted plagues and calamities brought forth against God's enemies, the idea of a passive God seems laughable. When we read about his grace without bounds and his unending mercy to those in Christ, it makes a God devoid of feeling an impossibility. And yet, as the oft-quoted axiom goes, "The opposite of love is not hate; it's indifference." Perhaps this is why apparent apathy from God cuts as deeply as it does. First John 4:8 plainly tells us that "God is love"; yet when we encounter a Creator who seems disengaged, uninterested, or unconcerned, it naturally causes us to call into question everything we believe to be true about the very nature of God. Our God is passionate, fiery, loving, fear-inducing, and dramatic. Even when God appears as a still, small voice, God is first preceded by a great wind, an earthquake, and a fire (1 Kings 19:11–13). The mere suggestion that God might be apathetic seems completely out of character.

Unfortunately, many people (especially women) are accused of being "too emotional," as if having deep feelings is a moral failing. There are numerous Christian books and sermons that propagate the message "You can't trust your emotions; you can only trust God," implying that the two things somehow cancel each other out. But if we believe that the Bible is right when it says God "created humankind in his image" (Gen. 1:27), then the universal human traits that we also have in common with the Divine must stem from God, including emotions. The way to counteract apathy is to generate great feeling; perhaps, when it seems God feels nothing, God is actually encouraging us to do the feeling for ourselves—to sit with the fear or the pain or the frustration—in order to discover another aspect of the Almighty.

Martha needed to pull her focus away from the stresses of her ministry back to the joy and wonder of it. Jesus needed her to remember why she began to follow him in the first place and the motivation behind her work.

Jesus's disciples in the boat needed to be reminded of the profound reach of his power. These were people who saw him miraculously heal the afflicted, raise the dead, drive out demons, and feed the multitudes, and yet even *they* took his divine abilities for granted and overlooked the profound implications of his messiahship. Watching Jesus quell the storm with just a few words caused them to marvel at his power and see him in a whole new light: "And they were filled with great awe and said to one another, 'Who then is this, that even the wind and the sea obey him?'" (Mark 4:41).

It's hard to imagine that Jesus did not notice Martha scurrying about in the background. Surely he was aware that the boat was being thrown about in the storm. And yet, in both cases, he deliberately chose not to act, almost as if he were intentionally provoking his followers to ask him, "Lord, don't you care?" When God fails to behave in the way we believe God should, that compels us to adjust our own perspective, to feel big emotions that shift us into a different mode of thinking. Rarely

> *When God fails to behave in the way we believe God should, that compels us to adjust our own perspective, to feel big emotions that shift us into a different mode of thinking.*

do we emerge from a period of great emotion unchanged. Feeling things—*really* feeling them, giving them a voice and a name and a focus—forces us to encounter a new facet of God.

Yet it is too easy and too convenient to simply declare that God's apparent indifference is intended to rouse us from our own, and leave the matter at that. While this certainly may be true in many cases, anyone who has ever cried out to the Lord over and over again for long periods of time knows that indifference is hardly the issue on their part. When the silence stretches on too long or the hoped-for resolution does not materialize, it's easy to feel as if God is at fault; after all, God is the one who has the power to intervene and has chosen not to act.

But it is worth considering whether these periods when God seems wholly unconcerned with our struggles are intended to remind us of exactly the *opposite* point—that these conflicts do not stem from God at all.

When we examine some of these stories closely, we see that there are actually two different issues at play: (1) the physical, immediate concern, and (2) the frustration with a lack of response. While they are closely linked, they are still separate conflicts. It is not Mary's lack of action that finally provokes Martha to speak; it's the fact that Jesus seems to be ignoring it. It is not the storm itself that passengers on the boat complain to Jesus about, but the fact that he doesn't seem to care about their plight. In both instances, there are two distinct sources of stress: a problematic circumstance and God's apparent indifference.

Perhaps in absence of a response, God is intentionally provoking us into an emotional reaction to stir us to life, to force us to name the unsolvable thing, to recognize that our physical needs and our spiritual needs are not that separate after all—and *God is also inviting us to recognize that our suffering does not stem from the Divine.* Please note, this is not simply another way of asking, "What is God trying to teach you through this?"; it is forcing us to divide the problem into clear causes. It's not that something awful is happening because God doesn't care; something awful is happening, and that is precisely why we are calling on God. God's inaction is not the cause of the suffering, thus we cannot lay the blame at God's feet. Even when we know intellectually that God is not at fault, emotionally it can be difficult not to want to throw all our anger, frustration, sadness, and feelings of betrayal in God's direction, pinning on the Almighty the consequences and unfair dealings of the natural course of life in a fallen world.

Maybe by driving us to ask, "Lord, don't you care?" God is inviting us to recognize that God exists independent of the struggle. It does not come from God, nor is God's authority impacted by it. We will never find comfort from the source of our pain; we cannot find peace in the very thing causing our conflict. When we cry out to God to do something, it reminds us that God is *not* the source of our suffering. Acknowledging divine inaction is actually our chance to absolve God of guilt; only then can we truly turn to God for comfort and peace. This does not mean that God will automatically make the circumstance better; while Jesus *did* calm the storm, he did *not* force Mary to get up and pitch in. But what he offered in both instances was a chance for authentic engagement, communication, and ultimately a deeper understanding of a different facet of his nature.

Maybe by driving us to ask, "Lord, don't you care?" God is inviting us to recognize that God exists independent of the struggle

o o o

It's been well over a decade since I realized my prayers were not enough to bring back my baby—not then and not the two other times it happened afterward. There are still days when I want to ask, "Lord, don't you care?" and still days when God's only answer is silence. But I have learned that simply the ability to ask means that I have not given up on hearing from God.

If you have found yourself asking the same question, it means that, despite all your (probably justifiable) anger, frustration, or sadness, you know God seems to be acting contrary to his nature. It means that your soul still recognizes God as all-powerful and all-loving. By allowing yourself to experience the honesty of those emotions, you are actually reinforcing the truth that God is good, God is caring, and God is love. If this were not true, *why would you expect a better response from* God? This realization may not lessen the pain or cause your frustration at the situation to fully subside, but perhaps it can divert your anger enough that you are still able to see God as a source of goodness and grace.

Or perhaps, at the very least, you may find that this is true: deep down—maybe so deep you aren't even consciously aware of it—there is still the belief that God is who God says God is. The Lord may not look anything like the way you've been taught to understand God, but if you can recognize the disconnect enough to ask the question "Lord, don't you care?" it means that instinctively you still acknowledge God is there. If you can accept the divine invitation to be in the moment and sit with that seed of belief, maybe you will eventually find a new starting point for fuller and more authentic engagement.

4

ATROPHY:
THE GOD WHO CAN'T SEEM TO ACT

Mark 15:29–32

The Neoplatonist philosopher Porphyry, originally from Tyre in Roman Syria, wrote extensively defending traditional pagan systems against the Christian religion that was spreading rapidly across the Mediterranean and Near East during the third century. One of Porphyry's main arguments against the validity of this relatively new, upstart faith was that Jesus's claims to be God could not be true based on his own apparent weakness. What sort of deity, Porphyry reasoned, would fail to take action to defend themselves or prove their own power? It must be either a very foolish or a very weak god, in which case they are hardly any god at all:

> Does Christ in the same way—being unable to drive the demons from his territory—send them as far as he can send them, namely into the unclean beasts [Matt. 8:28–34]? If so, he does indeed do something marvelous and worth talking about. But it is also the sort of action that raises questions about his divine powers.

A reasonable person, upon hearing such a tale, instinctively
makes up his mind as to the truthfulness of the story; he says
something like "If Christ does not do his good for the benefit of
everything under the sun, but only relocates the evil by driving
it from place to place, and if he takes care of some and neglects
others—well, what sort of good is he as a savior?"
—Porphyry, *Against the Christians*, c. 275–300 CE[1]

Porphyry cites a number of examples to support his challenge,
such as Jesus's silence before Pilate. He argues that if Jesus were
truly divine, he should have used the opportunity to convert his
accusers or speak wisdom to impress the crowd. "But, no," Porphyry writes, "he only manages to be whipped and spit on and
crowned with briars." Similarly, the philosopher argues, when
Jesus converses with Satan during his temptation, "he certainly
might have been willing to demonstrate that he could deliver
others first by throwing himself down from the heights without
hurting himself. . . . The honest thing for Jesus to have done would
be to demonstrate to those in the temple that he was God's son
and was able to deliver them as well as himself from danger."
Thus, Porphyry concludes, there is no logical reason to trust a
man who claims to be God but cannot even stop himself from
being "made fun of like a peasant boy in the big city."

Porphyry's criticism was rooted in the fact that Jesus's inaction at crucial moments in his story stacked far more evidence in
favor of Jesus as a weak imposter than as a strong, powerful deity.
He was not alone in raising these questions, of course, though he
may have been more blunt than others in their presentation. How
many of us have felt the same way, wondering why God's apparent inaction at crucial points in our own story fails to align with
the omnipotent deity we were taught about in Sunday school?
When the God we are promised can do everything doesn't seem
to do anything, we may find ourselves questioning whether God's
powers and loyalty were vastly oversold.

Jesus himself mentions that there were many starving widows in Israel during the days of Elijah, yet the prophet was only sent to help one woman, a foreigner (Luke 4:25-26). And why was healing only offered to the first person into the pool at Bethesda (John 5:4)? Why does Jesus not heal all the sick in Palestine? Why limit mercy? Why put a cap on God's power? The times when Jesus chooses to act and the times when he refrains may even seem illogical. As Porphyry writes: "When brought before the high priest and Roman governor, why didn't Jesus say anything to suggest he was wise or divine? He could have taught his judge and his accusers how to become better men! . . . And even if Christ's suffering was carried out according to God's plan, even if he was meant to suffer punishment—at least he might have faced his suffering nobly and spoken words of power and wisdom to Pilate."

Of course, Porphyry wasn't the first person to raise such questions. Such challenges were raised even in the midst of Jesus's trial and crucifixion. The Jewish high priest, trying to make sense of the evidence laid before him, questions Jesus, who steadfastly refuses to respond in any way that would help his own case: "The high priest stood up and said, 'Have you no answer? What is it that they testify against you?' But Jesus was silent" (Matt. 26:62-63). The audience at the cross takes it even further, ordering Jesus to save himself if he really is the Son of God. When he fails to respond to their challenges, they laugh at him as if he were a child or a braggart making outrageous claims he is unable to back up: "Those who passed by derided him, shaking their heads and saying, 'Aha! You who would destroy the temple and build it in three days, save yourself, and come down from the cross!' In the same way the chief priests, along with the scribes, were also mocking him among themselves and saying, 'He saved others; he cannot save himself. Let the Messiah, the King of Israel, come down from the cross now, so that we may see and believe.' Those who were crucified with him also taunted him" (Mark 15:29-32).

These doubts are not unreasonable; after all, Jesus's refusal
to act can easily be read as impotence rather than restraint. We
may scorn the mockers when we read this passage in our Bibles,
angry that they would be so disrespectful to Jesus. Yet we often
do something similar, demanding to know why God has failed to
act in our circumstances when so many others were given delivery. It can be deeply discouraging and even unsettling when we
hear stories of miraculous interventions but fail to experience
our own. How do we respond when it feels like we invested our
faith in a God who is out of miracles?

The uncomfortable reality is that many of us built our theologies on a prosperity gospel merely rebranded under a number of
different titles: the "Christian political agenda," *#blessed*, the purity movement, or any of a dozen other doctrines that we somehow
conflated with the gospel. Even though we may reject the notion
that we are operating under a "seed faith" or "health and wealth"
theology, the fact is that many churches have presented the Christian life as an if-then proposition: *If you follow this acceptable formula for your life, then God will bless you.* Even though the "deal"
might not be tied to literal prosperity, the principle is the same:

If we all vote a certain way, then God will pour out favor on
the country.

If you enjoy material wealth, then it must be a direct result of your
faithfulness to God.

If you guard your virginity until your wedding night, then God will
give you a healthy, conflict-free marriage.

If you pray hard enough, then God will deliver you from your painful circumstance.

If you work hard, then God will reward you with success.

It's ironclad; the only thing between us and a better life is the
strength of our faith, so we establish scenarios in which we seem

to think God is obliged to act when and how we want. Yet in so doing, we essentially reduce the Creator of the universe to a wish-granting genie or a benevolent Santa Claus who will continue to shower us with blessings as long as we stay on the "nice list." We gauge God's power by what God has done for us, good or bad. In this way, our faith becomes little more than a transactional relationship whereby we "pay" for measurable metrics (which we call "blessings") with prayer, good deeds, evangelism, and trust. Ultimately, we measure the "effectiveness" of our faith by what God does to close the formula we opened and expected God to fulfill. In anthropology, this kind of practice is called "magical thinking," where the performance of a certain behavior or ritual will conjure a specific result or bring supernatural favor on an individual or situation. It is a way of asserting control over circumstances to achieve a desired, predictable outcome. Few of us would admit to believing that we can control God by our actions, and yet how many of us engage in this type of practice in the hopes that God will prove to be manipulatable after all?

In chapter 3, we discussed two stories where God's failure to act prompted an indignant response. Martha challenges Jesus for his apparent indifference to her exhaustive and thankless ministry efforts (Luke 10:40). Likewise, in the midst of a storm, Jesus's disciples demand, "Teacher, do you not care that we are perishing?" (Mark 4:38). We already know the endings of the stories—Jesus praises Mary and quells the storm—so we often push past the accusations to get to the resolution. Yet this kind of easy, outcome-based theology that focuses on the "deliverables" is small comfort when we are the person stuck in the middle of the story, wondering when and how—and sometimes even *if*—God can act. There is no silence more deafening than the silence of unanswered prayers. We don't want to wait; we want answers.

Our Western, capitalist understanding of life tends to be results oriented. We want to know the bottom line before we decide if something is worth the investment. Unfortunately, we also tend to extend this principle to God, viewing a lack of divine intervention as a sign of weakness or, worse, inability. We talk about the importance of "bearing fruit" in our spiritual lives as if the harvest matters more than the cultivation process. Yet the theology on which so many of us were raised is rooted in a *deus ex machina* mentality—literally "God from the machine." This plot device has its roots in ancient Greek theater, when a seemingly hopeless situation was suddenly resolved by the unlikely appearance of a deity to quickly and neatly solve the problem. The expression stems from the fact that the actor playing the role of the god or goddess was usually brought onstage by means of a machine such as a primitive crane or a mechanical trapdoor, and has since come to mean any resolution that comes out of nowhere and ties everything up with a neat bow.

How many "preacher stories" have we heard of ministries in desperate straits that received an unexpected check in the mail on the very day the mortgage was due? Or lessons in devotional books describing someone whose cancer disappeared after an intensive prayer session at church? Or callers on Christian radio who admit to being suicidal until the perfect song plays over the airwaves? How many times have we seen these types of stories celebrated as evidence of God and coupled with the implied or even overt message that "This deliverance can be yours, too, if you just turn your life over to Christ"?

But how many of us have ever pinned our hopes on a miracle, only to be left with disappointment? How many of us have felt cheated when our eleventh-hour deliverance, or that of a loved one, never arrived? It's not that we begrudge others their miraculous story, it's just that—well, *why didn't we get one, too*? If the gospel we learn is wrapped in the promise that God will always come to our aid, what happens to our belief when God fails to show up in any recognizable form? A missionary friend once remarked to me, "You have to remember that those things—Christian radio and evangelical books—they're all propaganda. That's how you pique someone's interest and draw them in. You have to get their attention with the promise. You can't talk about the nuance until later." The problem is, when you start with a false premise, the entire foundation becomes unstable and people begin to question whether any of it is true.

This is the very issue I discussed with Charles, a widower who recently retired from a forty-year government career, including twenty years as a submariner in the navy. A preacher's kid who himself has served as an elder in his church for more than three decades, Charles now works in pastoral care at a hospital as a secular chaplain—not because he has abandoned his faith but because "non-Christians are the more open-minded people. . . . We talk about the power of forgiveness and brokenness. It's amazing how effective I feel I can be in speaking to the principles of Jesus without even invoking Christianity, which has so many negative connotations for so many people."

One of the challenges Charles encounters regularly both in his work at the hospital and in his church is people who feel let down by the fact that life does not seem to have played out for them the way they were promised. People from a religious background often feel as if they were oversold on a promise of God that couldn't live up to the hype. Charles sees a great deal of disillusionment, especially among young adults, at the idea that whatever cosmic deals were in place for previous generations don't seem to be in effect anymore. "The rewards systems and, frankly, traditions, just aren't panning out for them like they did for a generation or two after World War I and World War II, when we thought we had 'The Dream,'" he explains.

> We had cutting-edge science and "God Bless America" was a kind of manifest destiny. So the dream that my parents and their parents had told them was, "This is what success looks like." But it doesn't apply to twenty-five year olds today. Somehow, just working hard doesn't seem to be the answer to every-

thing that it once was. People say, "That's another faith-fallacy that doesn't sit right with me. I work hard, but look what I'm getting." . . .

I am thankful for who that generation was and what they did, but there are so many constructs that they were a part of that I can't adhere to today and I can't express to others, especially younger folks, because institutional religion in the '50s, '60s, and '70s—the whole postwar period—was more about "look what we can do" and "the more we do, the better we are" and "in the end you'll get these rewards." That's just not reality for a lot of people.

What we are witnessing right now with so many people leaving the church or deconstructing their faith is, in large part, a pushback against the sort of nationalist thinking that infiltrated Western Christianity in the last two hundred years. As manufacturing sectors and economies grew, it was easy to equate hard work with morality. This is, after all, the philosophy behind the so-called Protestant work ethic, a phrase first coined early in the twentieth century by German sociologist and economist Max Weber. The idea is that human labor is an inseparable part of the Christian ethos. In itself, this is not necessarily a problematic or outrageous suggestion, considering biblical passages such as Adam's curse to work the land (Gen. 3:17-19); the parable of the talents, whereby servants are rewarded based on the yield they produce by investing for their master (Matt. 25:14-30); and verses such as "Anyone unwilling to work should not eat" (2 Thess. 3:10). The problem, however, is that many people in the Christian-dominated West equated their nation's growing prosperity with its religious activity. Missionaries and church planters continued to export their own cultural values as they had done for generations, only now the impact was accelerated by the additional influence of American media and manufacturing. Consumption and abundance seemed to herald the favor of God. Given that communism (with its antireligious stance) was on the rise elsewhere in the world in the mid-twentieth century, the result was a conflation, in many Christian institutions, of God's favor with capitalism. The harder we work, the more God blesses us. Nowhere is this theology better encapsulated, perhaps, than in the popular Sunday school song "The Wise Man and the Foolish Man," written by Ann Omley in 1948. After describing how each man builds his house on either the Rock or the sand, and how the life built on the Rock withstands falling rain and rising floods, the final verse launches into a refrain that repeats: "So build your life on the Lord Jesus Christ, / And the blessings will come down. / The blessings come down as your prayers go up, / The blessings come down as your prayers go up. . . . So build your life on the Lord."

By incentivizing faith—not just in terms of the promise of heaven but also in our world here and now—we have found a means of trying to control God or bending God to our will. The message that many of us were inadvertently taught was that by working/praying/believing hard enough, we create a situation in which God is contractually obligated to respond. We conveniently overlook Scriptures about camels and the needle's eye, and we start to view God's blessings as a kind of honest profit because we have reduced our relationship with God to a business venture. Of course, most preachers would deny promoting any such view from the pulpit, and yet we teach our children about trading prayers for blessings in Cradle Roll. We've confused economic principles with religious ones, but our cultural identity is so wrapped up in the two complementing one another that we are unsure of how to untangle them.

We've confused economic principles with religious ones, but our cultural identity is so wrapped up in the two complementing one another that we are unsure of how to untangle them.

When we equate the accrual of material goods with God's favor or believe that we merit a payoff for following a formula, we are inadvertently teaching the reverse as well: that God will take back or withhold those rewards from anyone who does not stick to the script. Of course, it is true that people may face consequences for their choices and God may not intervene, but it is very difficult to justify this kind of simplistic cause-and-effect thinking to people who *did* stick to the script. Try to sell the idea of "earned blessings" to those who followed the teachings of purity culture to the letter, because they were told that was the only way to have a God-pleasing family, and ten years later, are engaged in conversations about custody and alimony while their supposedly godless friends who lived together before their wedding are enjoying a rock-solid marriage and a weekend at the beach with their picture-perfect children.

See how the "pray to play" ideology goes over with the humble, hardworking individual who poured everything into building a business—tithing to the local church and operating with scrupulous ethics—just to watch a life's work go under during pandemic restrictions while another boastful, crude mogul rides out the lockdowns with a little creative accounting and not a single sleepless night.

How do you justify this kind of God to a grieving family who just lost a loved one to suicide after years of struggling, pleading for help, begging for divine intervention, visiting counselors and therapists, and trying different medications for mental health challenges? How do you maintain a theology rooted in the belief that God rewards hard work when all that hard work still culminated in an empty chair at the table and a thousand unanswered prayers?

No wonder an entire generation of believers is questioning the very premise of the Western church and the various cultural and political alliances it has made. Those who have chosen to stay in the church often find themselves struggling with cognitive dissonance. What they are seeing and hearing from the church is not how they are experiencing God, so many feel their only option is to throw out old ideas of an Almighty and reconsider what it is they *are* actually dealing with. They are fed up with the spiritual gaslighting that tries to pin their success or failure in life on how closely they toe the party line, even when evidence to the contrary is all around.

So, what happened? Did God simply burn out? Does each individual have a withdrawal limit on God's power? Or maybe God needs *us* to stick to whatever formula we've assigned a situation in order to intervene; maybe God's literally dependent on us completing certain steps before divine action is possible. Of course, it sounds absurd spelled out in such blatant terms, reducing God to a battery or grace to an ATM or prayer to the quarter in the slot that fires up the celestial pinball machine. Yet how else are we to wrap our minds around inaction from a God who is supposedly all-knowing and all-loving?

The Gospels are filled with stories of Jesus restoring sight to the blind and health to the lepers, but what about the people Jesus didn't heal? In numerous instances we are told that Jesus cured all the sick who were brought to him, but in John 5 we see "many invalids" lying at the pool of Bethesda—yet Jesus seems to have tended to only one man that day. It seems unlikely that Jesus failed to notice those other souls languishing in their sickness, and yet he did not restore them all to health. So, what happened? Did he love one person more than the others? Or was he sapped after that particular healing and needed to recharge? And what about the mourners at Lazarus's funeral, who asked amongst themselves, "Could not he who opened the eyes of the blind man have kept this man from dying?" (John 11:37). The real questions the mourners were asking were, *Is God really who God says God is? And, if so, why is God not acting in these circumstances?*

But Jesus did act at Bethesda and at Lazarus's grave; even for the people he didn't heal and even before he restored Lazarus to life, God at least showed up. Even when God didn't speak up on God's own behalf or save God's own self from the cross, God was still present. Ultimately, then, the issue is not that God failed to act but that God failed to act *in the way we expected God to act.* Most of us have been taught, by osmosis if not by direct teaching, that God's people will always come out on top. We say we know things don't always work in our favor, but in our hearts it still feels unjust because of how we have been conditioned to believe God operates. In the end, we often blame God for failing to live up to our standards when God doesn't show up the way we think God should.

Only when we release our expectations of the Almighty can we allow God to operate beyond the restrictions of our demands. We must divorce ourselves from the desire to control or manipulate God by trapping the Creator of the universe in a reciprocal contract whose terms we established ourselves. But just as importantly, we must put our faith in God rather than in the outcome. Instead of acting as if there were a way to "hack God" by applying a formula that God is obliged to follow or believing that God can only act if we offer up enough of the right kinds of

We must put our faith in God rather than in the outcome.

prayers and good works, we must be willing to accept that we cannot place God in our debt. We have to disconnect from the rebranded prosperity gospel lens through which we have been culturally conditioned to see life; otherwise, we are simply creating God in our own image and blaming or doubting when God doesn't comply.

It can be deeply unsettling to abandon a rewards-based understanding of God because the entire concept is so deeply ingrained in the way most of us have been trained to understand the world and our place in it. We think of blessings as the things we deserve, and suffering as injustice, spiritual persecution, or God's inadequacy. In short, we have developed an entitlement mentality that elevates outcomes into idols.

Unfortunately, there is no easy way to overturn this message that has undergirded so much of our fundamental understanding of the cosmic laws of the universe. The first step, though, is to recognize it and name it for what it is. It is not weakness or failure or inadequacy on God's part; it is a misguided and misapplied doctrine that has found a home within so many of our churches because it is such an easy and convenient means of validation and control. No matter how noble our intentions may be— and there is nothing wrong with wanting healing or a satisfying marriage or a resolution to an ongoing struggle—faith is more than a formula. We must not pin our beliefs on whatever we have been taught

We think of blessings as the things we deserve, and suffering as injustice, spiritual persecution, or God's inadequacy.

to believe we are owed or else we are little different from Porphyry, the high priest, or the mockers at the cross who only got silence when they expected a show.

You have the right and the power to take back your faith from those people and ideas who want to reduce God to a predictable result, like a chemical reaction, or that limit God's strength, creativity, and grace by hemming God in with a predetermined standard of acceptability. When we release our faith from the culturally conditioned expectations of other people, we give ourselves permission to find the Divine in the ways God wishes to reveal God's self rather than missing God because God did not show up as we imagined. It may not bring deliverance, it may not ease the pain, but it does mean that your faith is your own instead of a set of small-minded or limited beliefs unwittingly inherited from generations past.

5

ANGER:
THE GOD OF PUNISHMENT

> *Joshua 7*
> *Job 42:7–9*
> *Luke 13:1–8*
> *Romans 14*

Since the Plymouth Colony, the American Protestant church has rooted its identity in creating order out of chaos. On the ragged edge of a wild continent, the first European settlers sought to build a "shining city on a hill" from the scant farms and towns scratched out of the land they claimed as their own.

Adam's curse meant that humanity's relationship with a fallen, broken world was defined through our own responsibility and culpability for our sins. We suffered because we deserved to suffer, and any circumstance could be overcome with enough faith, prayer, and penitence. The great mysteries of the divine order, such as why bad things happen to good people, were simply explained away through a combination of God's sovereign will and humanity's sinful nature.

This mindset laid the groundwork for multiple great revivals on the frontier and in the burgeoning cities. It was the backbone of the self-help industry that caught steam in the twentieth century. It is at the heart of the prosperity gospel. It is proclaimed from countless evangelical pulpits every Sunday: the only thing standing between you and a life rich with profound fulfillment and connection to God is *your sin.*

When something bad happens, we look for causes, for reasons, for explanations as to what our part was in the mess—what we did to set us up for this pain or what we had to learn from it to purify our character. It is almost as if we have forgotten that, every day, the collateral damage of a fallen world shows up without rhyme, reason, or religious imperative. Jesus reminds his followers of this in Luke 13. When one of them reported to Jesus about a desecration of some sacrifices that the governor Pilate had committed, Jesus asks, "Do you think that because these Galileans suffered in this way they were worse sinners than all other Galileans?" (13:2). Then he adds a comment about another recent event Luke's contemporary readership was likely to recognize: "Or those eighteen who were killed when the tower of Siloam fell on them—do you think that they were worse offenders than all the others living in Jerusalem?" In this same passage, Jesus encourages his followers to repent of their sins, but he takes pains to point out that not every catastrophe is the direct result of sin. Chaos happens. Innocent bystanders become casualties in the brokenness of life. It's not fair, but it's also not evidence that God is angry with any of the parties involved.

Unfortunately, an all-too-common response in religious circles is to ask the suffering individual whether they have any unresolved sin that could be the cause of such a punishment. Not only is this victim blaming, it's reaching down to pick up a rock at Jesus's charge: "Let anyone among you who is without sin be the first to throw a stone" (John 8:7). Who doesn't have sin in their life? And yet how quick we often are to assign someone else's struggles to their sin while ascribing our own to simply being tested or tried in our faith.

Allison was a college freshman when she was sexually assaulted at a New Year's Eve party. The response she got from her family and church community afterward led her to question everything she thought she understood about her faith: "I had been drinking, and people seemed to act like that explained it. The people preaching God, who are supposed to be there to protect you, the church family that is supposed to be beside you no matter what? I didn't really experience that. I remember my mom asking me a few weeks later, 'Are you an alcoholic? You've never touched it before in your life.' I know my parents wanted me to be okay and get help, but [the drinking] was a big focus point for them like it was a reason for what happened." When Allison's parents urged her to move nearer to home and transfer to a Christian college, in the hopes the support would help her move on, she encountered a similar response: "I would try to open up to people about my assault, but as soon as I got to the fact that there was drinking at a party, people got uncomfortable and a lot less sympathetic. It's not a great way to heal when people are actually pushing you away. . . . What happened to me and the fact that I was 'sinning that night,' as people liked to remind me—if Jesus had heard me talking and trying to connect, that never would have been his reaction."

Sadly, Allison's experiences are not unique; as many of us can attest, they are actually frighteningly common. Any time a new crisis looms, be it hurricanes or COVID-19, it seems some religious leader or another grabs headlines to proclaim that the current events are a direct result of God seeking to punish the country for turning away from righteousness. It's an easy way to establish an us-versus-them dichotomy, where "we" are the righteous who recognize the vengeance of the Lord upon "those other people" who aren't living up to God's standards. This logic starts to break down, however, when we are faced with images of churches hanging up plywood over their broken windows or crisis pregnancy centers bailing water out of their lobbies or food pantries going unstaffed due to an outbreak of a pandemic among their staff. If

God is lashing out from anger, there certainly seems to be little heavenly concern for collateral damage. It's small comfort to remind people of Jesus's words in Matthew 5:45, that God "makes his sun rise on the evil and on the good, and sends rain on the righteous and on the unrighteous," when days before we insisted this was all part of a divine punishment. It's unconscionable to tell a child, "You reap whatever you sow" (Gal. 6:7), as they stand beside the ruins of their home in the aftermath of a natural disaster.

Yet this kind of response to a troubling or scary set of circumstances persists because it is a convenient way to make a bold pronouncement that is impossible to disprove; after all, when was the last time God sat down for an interview with the evening news to outline divine reasoning? It is rhetorically problematic when people speak authoritatively on matters they don't understand. Circumstances can shift in ways they can't foresee or anticipate, and the result is often a conviction by one's own words.

Kurt, a college professor and deacon in his church, describes his childhood in an evangelical church in 1970s Texas. It was filled with loving, well-meaning people, but the view of God he encountered there was extremely narrow. He struggled with the apparent inconsistencies or glossed-over parts of Bible stories. "I had a very hazy understanding of how God intervenes in our lives in prayer. I was told things like 'The effective, fervent prayer of a righteous man availeth much, so get to praying and you can move mountains' and 'Whatever you ask for in prayer, believing, you shall receive.' That's how prayer works," he explains.

Then, as a student at a conservative Christian college, he recalls when a theology professor brought up the story of Rahab and the spies from Joshua 1:

> He said, "Scholars disagree why those spies went to Rahab's house. Some people say that God led them there. And some people say it was an accident. And some people say they went to Rahab's house for the same reason all men went to Rahab's house."

There were about three beats of silence as he stared at us
and we stared at him, and I'm sure my eyes became gigantic as
I realized the implications of what he was saying. I felt a surge
of anger, like "Wait a minute. WAIT. Are you telling me that God
can work through men going to a whorehouse?" . . . That was
the starting place of me revising my understanding of how God
interacts with people—even how God interacts with his people.

This moment set Kurt on a path of reevaluating just how tit-for-
tat God really was, and it came at a time when this same question
was being posed somewhat differently to society at-large:

It was the early '80s, and people had started saying, "You know,
there is a disease that is spreading through the gay community and it is killing them." That disease was originally called
"GRID"—gay-related immunodeficiency—but they had to
change that when all of a sudden people who weren't gay were
getting it. . . . Churches had said, "Well, that's just God taking
revenge on people who are behaving in abominable ways." And
that argument lasted for several years until so many other people started dying—people who were not gay. And people then
had to revise "How God worked in the world."

And I was watching all of this happen because my own
brother was dying of AIDS.

Condemnation is easy and convenient until it no longer fits the
narrative those in power have created. How easy it is to say, "God
is acting in this way because of _____." There is no answerabil-
ity, no checks and balances, no one to tell us we are wrong. Jesus
even hits on a related point when he challenges the Pharisees, "For
which is easier, to say, 'Your sins are forgiven,' or to say, 'Stand
up and walk'?" (Matt. 9:5). The lack of hard evidence from the
spiritual realm regarding God's mindset makes ascribing actions
to God far easier than any sort of statement that can actually be

verified. Who can say for sure what God's motives are for certain circumstances or whether someone's sins have actually been forgiven? With no means of measurement, there is no accountability, which means this is one of the easiest and also most easily abused means of asserting authority. And perhaps no one in the Bible illustrates this point better than Job's three friends, Eliphaz the Temanite, Bildad the Shuhite, and Zophar the Naamathite.

When we are faced with a period of seemingly unjust or inexplicable trials, well-meaning church people seem inevitably to make at least a passing reference to Job, a deeply polarizing story. To some, Job is an inspiring figure of fortitude and perseverance; to others, his story is a hackneyed guilt trip about how things could always be worse. However the book strikes you, there is one detail we often seem to overlook: we are privy to knowledge Job never receives. We are afforded a glimpse into debates in the heavenly realms that set forth the terms of the "bet," but Job is never given that privilege. As a result, we have a lens for understanding and framing the events that Job was denied. From this perspective—a God's-eye view of the situation rather than an earthly one—it is easy to forget that Job was never offered a reason for his suffering. He never understood what was gained by his losses; he only knew that God had reasons for allowing his suffering to come to pass, and that was all. And yet that did not stop Eliphaz, Bildad, and Zophar from dropping by to offer their take on his plight.

At first, their presence is innocuous—even compassionate. When they arrive, they say nothing; instead "They sat with him on the ground seven days and seven nights, and no one spoke a word to him, for they saw that his suffering was very great" (Job 2:13). As so often is the case, it is not until well-meaning religious folk open their mouths that the trouble begins. One by one, they begin to challenge Job, initially cloaking their statements in compliments before launching into a series of accusations challenging Job to identify, confess to, and uproot some hidden sin in

his life that is the cause of what could only be a divine punishment. Job defends himself, insisting that he has done his best to
pursue justice, deal fairly, and act uprightly, making amends for
his sins when they occur. He even challenges his friends' authority to levy such accusations against him, asking,

> "How forceful are honest words!
>   But your reproof, what does it reprove?
> Do you think that you can reprove words,
>   as if the speech of the desperate were wind?"
>
> (6:25–26)

Finally, late in the text, a fourth friend, Elihu, joins Job and his
companions. But unlike the other three, when Elihu finally
speaks up, he does so with a seemingly different motive. We are
told, "He was angry at Job because he justified himself rather than
God; he was angry also at Job's three friends because they had
found no answer, though they had declared Job to be in the
wrong" (32:2–3). Elihu makes his own blanket pronouncements
regarding the nature of suffering, but he stops short of accusing
Job of angering God. Significantly, in Job 42:7–9, when God speaks
in anger against Job's accusatory friends, Elihu alone is not
named. It appears the Lord reserved wrath only for those who
used God's name to condemn others.

It appears the Lord reserved wrath only for those who used God's name to condemn others.

So often, it seems that people who
are eager to attribute pain to God's
anger are really revealing something
of their own issues through what psychologists call "projection," in which
one party casts their own issues onto
someone else, and then claims to see the struggles in the other
person. It is a textbook behavior in gaslighting, and it happens in
our churches and ministries every day when leaders rail about
materialism while owning private jets, preach exhaustively about

the trap of sexual immorality while privately engaging in sexual misconduct, accuse young women of driving men to lust without holding men accountable for their own thoughts, or simply gossiping about how much other people gossip. It's almost a cliché that the religious or political leader who is the most outspoken against rights for same-sex couples turns out to have an active private life in the gay community. This kind of hypocritical projection was even true among Jesus's disciples. Consider how angry Judas got about Mary spending an exorbitant sum on perfume to anoint Jesus's feet—money he insists could have been used to feed the needy—when, as John adds in a parenthetical remark in his gospel: "(He said this not because he cared about the poor, but because he was a thief; he kept the common purse and used to steal what was put into it)" (12:6).

It is human nature to read our own guilt onto other people. At best, we do so simply because it is the lens through which we see and understand; but we also do it hoping it deflects attention away from our own shortcomings in that same area or even in order to maintain our own sense of superiority. Take, for example, the story of Michal in 2 Samuel 6. When David, the newly crowned king of Israel, returns with the ark of the covenant after fighting back the Philistines, he dances wildly in celebration in a manner that his wife (and Saul's daughter) Michal finds embarrassing and undignified because his robes seem to have flown up, exposing him to the crowd. She greets him, saying, "How the king of Israel honored himself today, uncovering himself today before the eyes of his servants' maids, as any vulgar fellow might shamelessly uncover himself!" (6:20).

David responds with equal contempt, telling Michal: "It was before the LORD, who chose me in place of your father and all his household, to appoint me as prince over Israel, the people of the LORD, that I have danced before the LORD. I will make myself yet more contemptible than this, and I will be abased in my own eyes; but by the maids of whom you have spoken, by them I shall be held in honor" (6:21–22). And then one simple sentence concludes the incident: "And Michal the daughter of Saul had no child to the day of her death" (6:23).

This story has been featured in many sermons to warn listeners against criticizing God's appointed leaders. It is discussed at length in many essays and support groups for infertility. It crops up in debates about worship style, when one group is critical of the style another group prefers. Each time, the takeaway seems to be the same: God withheld children from Michal as punishment for her attitude toward David.

Except that the text never says that at all. There is no connection cited between Michal's annoyance and her infertility, no divine closing of her womb out of anger for her chastisement of her husband. It simply is not there, and yet this passage is commonly used as a prooftext to dissuade the laity from challenging the leadership, as a way to blame the pain of childlessness on women who "aren't submissive enough," and as a means of shutting down discussion within the church when someone seeks to question the way worship is conducted. Those who point to this story as a warning are wielding the supposed wrath of God to control people who might pose a threat to the established authority. By repeating the lesson often and loudly, they've managed to convince people to see something in the text that actually is not there at all. That is gaslighting in its purest form.

There are other ways, too, that people pass their own issues on to us, such as through an abusive childhood, a dysfunctional relationship, or social guilt. When we absorb or inherit spiritual anxiety or shame as a result of our upbringing, peer group, or religious background, we are being inflicted with scars from wounds that were never our fault. Remember that Scripture encourages us to help others with their struggles but never to bear the brunt of them ourselves. When others try to place their issues, stories, hang-ups, and encumbrances on us, they are standing in the way of the resurrection. We were not created to bear the punishment for other people's sins; only Christ can do that.

It's never too late to set that vicarious burden down. It's okay to say, "This millstone doesn't belong to me. It's yours, and you may take it back."

• • •

One of the most striking examples of God's anger as a direct cause of divine punishment is in Joshua 7, after the sacking of Jericho. Despite an explicit warning to the troops not to take a single item in plunder, one soldier named Achan disobeys, stashing an exquisite garment and a hoard of gold and silver beneath his tent. When the Israelites launch a subsequent attack on the city of Ai, they fail miserably, and Joshua is desperate to understand why God's favor suddenly seems to have been lifted from them. The text tells us: "Then Joshua tore his clothes, and fell to the ground on his face before the ark of the LORD until the evening, he and the elders of Israel; and they put dust on their heads" (7:6). He cries out to God for an explanation, and God replies in a somewhat surprising way: "The LORD said to Joshua, 'Stand up! Why have you fallen upon your face? Israel has sinned; they have transgressed my covenant that I imposed on them. They have taken some of the devoted things; they have stolen, they have acted deceitfully, and they have put them among their own belongings'" (7:10-11).

We were not created to bear the punishment for other people's sins; only Christ can do that.

God's first reaction to Joshua and all the elders falling prostrate is not to say, "That's right. Your nation has angered me, and here's what I'm going to do about it." Instead, God's response is to order them to their feet and to ask why they are groveling with their faces in the dirt. In other words, God is telling them, "The sin isn't yours. You are not the ones who need to be apologizing. You do, however, need to stand up and take action."

The guilty party is swiftly identified and condemned, along with his entire household, in a systematic process of elimination by which God points out the culprit to the leaders of Israel:

> Then Joshua and all Israel with him took Achan son of Zerah,
> with the silver, the mantle, and the bar of gold, with his sons
> and daughters, with his oxen, donkeys, and sheep, and his tent
> and all that he had; and they brought them up to the Valley of
> Achor. Joshua said, "Why did you bring trouble on us? The LORD
> is bringing trouble on you today." And all Israel stoned him to
> death; they burned them with fire, cast stones on them, and
> raised over him a great heap of stones that remains to this day.
> Then the LORD turned from his burning anger. Therefore that
> place to this day is called the Valley of Achor ["Achor" means
> "trouble"]. (7:24-26)

It is impossible to regard this passage as anything other than
deeply problematic to any basic sense of humanity. Theologians
(of both the credentialed and armchair variety) have performed
rather impressive feats of ethical, logical, and apologetic gymnastics to explain away the gruesome and unjust ending to this
story, but there is little that can make this story sit well with
modern readers. Nor should it. There is no smoothing over the
horror and injustice of what happened to Achan's household, and
to ignore that fact or to attempt to explain it away is intellectually
dishonest. In fact, people who leave their faith behind often cite
passages like these to justify why they cannot go on serving a God
who would condone such violence to innocent people.

This is exactly the challenge Portia experienced when she
raised these questions to several different pastors. In an online
forum I attended, several former believers spoke about their reasons for leaving the church. Portia, who agreed to let me share
her words, said this: "Whenever I asked honest questions about
violence or genocide, I was brushed off or fed simplistic explanations that were supposed to be enough, so that I finally decided
that if the church leaders and teachers could not be humble or
honest enough to say, 'I don't know, but I agree that it seems awful,' then what else were they lying to themselves about?"

With that in mind, we must acknowledge that there is no "comfortable" response to certain stories of God's wrath, and we *should* feel a sense of moral outrage when we read about the fate of Achan's family—just as we should feel a sense of moral outrage at anyone who does not recognize how deeply problematic that passage and others like it are. In fact, this is the *only* godly response. In Ezekiel 18, the prophet announces: "The word of the LORD came to me: What do you mean by repeating this proverb concerning the land of Israel, 'The parents have eaten sour grapes, and the children's teeth are set on edge'? As I live, says the Lord GOD, this proverb shall no more be used by you in Israel. Know that all lives are mine; the life of the parent as well as the life of the child is mine: it is only the person who sins that shall die" (18:1–4). If God himself has an issue with divine wrath being used to condemn innocent parties, surely we are permitted to be in agreement.

A near-universal story among the disability community is that religious family members or even perfect strangers often approach them and ask to pray that they might have the faith to be healed. Not only does this imply that life with a disability is somehow their fault, it also implies that their life is somehow "less than" exactly as it is, so *of course* they would change it if they could. Rather than allowing individuals with disabilities to make their own value judgments regarding their perceived limitations or even their personhood, some people of faith insist that wheelchairs, hearing devices, and neurodivergence are indications of God's punishment either for sin or for a lack of faith. Those with the audacity to feel within their rights to tell visually impaired individuals, people using leg braces, or the parents of children with autism that their condition is evidence of God's judgment obviously understand nothing about Jesus.

Let us not forget that the people Jesus physically healed *came to him*; he did not presume to force healing on anyone not seeking it. When he did approach people, he asked them first. In John 5,

Jesus talks to a man at the pool of Bethesda who has been ill for thirty-eight years. He could have snapped his fingers and changed the man's body in an instant, but instead he asked, "Do you want to be made well?" (5:6).

This exchange is often pointed to as an example of how we must be participants in our own salvation—we must *want* to be healed before Jesus can complete his work in us. But rhetorically, this line of thinking links the man's illness with sin; it equates his atypical physical condition with moral failings. Even though the connection between disability and sin is (usually) not intentional, this kind of equivalency reinforces the idea that disabilities are somehow retribution for wrongdoing. It is an easy trap in ableist thinking to automatically assume that healing equals eradicating the disability rather than allowing individuals to find salvation in their own spiritual journey.

What Jesus does in John 5 is to respect the man's personhood first by *asking* if he wanted physical healing instead of just taking for granted that he did. He recognized the man's differences but also the man's agency. In doing so, Jesus affirmed the man's humanity and wholeness exactly as he was. In John 9, Jesus and his disciplines encounter a man described as being "blind from birth." His disciples ask him, "Rabbi, who sinned, this man or his parents, that he was born blind?" Jesus answers, "Nei-

Disabled bodies do not exist for the sake of sermon illustrations or to be fetishized by an ableist theology.

ther this man nor his parents sinned; he was born blind so that God's works might be revealed in him" (John 9:1-3). In other words, the individual is, again, *already* a vessel of God's glory exactly as he is. Disabled bodies do not exist for the sake of sermon illustrations or to be fetishized by an ableist theology. Human beings are not billboards of God's wrath or object lessons in divine retribution.

If you are facing a change in your physical condition or you've recently learned that your child will not have the kind of life you envisioned due to a physical challenge or neurodivergence, you don't need a book to tell you that you are completely within your rights to feel whatever you want to. You don't have to celebrate a difficult diagnosis to be a faithful Christian, but neither does it mean that this is somehow God's revenge for sin in your life or evil in the world. Anyone who tries to shame you with such dubious and medieval reasoning as to say that Parkinson's disease or cerebral palsy is a sure sign of divine anger can hardly be trusted on more complex matters of faith.

Such obscene ableism stems from the offending individual's own limited view of what makes a person "whole," and this projecting of insecurities onto someone else unfortunately runs rampant in faith circles. In Romans 14, Paul makes the oft-cited argument that those who have more permissive faiths should not act in ways that cause those with more restrictive faiths to struggle. It is a favorite passage of people who wish to control or manipulate anyone with whom they disagree: "If your brother or sister is being injured by what you eat, you are no longer walking in love. Do not let what you eat cause the ruin of one for whom Christ died" (14:15). Applying that passage in isolation, however, ignores the greater context of the chapter, including, "Why do you pass judgment on your brother or sister? Or you, why do you despise your brother or sister? For we will all stand before the judgment seat of God" (14:10) and "So do not let your good be spoken of as evil" (14:16). In other words, do not project your issues onto others; they answer to God independent of your opinions. And, conversely, do not let anyone tell you that you are somehow in the wrong when you know that is not true. You alone are answerable to God for your life. Do not believe that your challenges or experiences outside of what is broadly considered "normal" are the result of God's displeasure with you just because someone told you so.

∘ ∘ ∘

This whole conversation, of course, is not to say that God never responds in anger or that sins do not carry consequences; we know from Scripture and experience that both are true. But it is a warning to think twice before giving credence to those whose immediate reaction to pain, struggle, or even just differences in our lives is to insist that they can interpret God's anger with authority and wield it as a threat, a weapon, or a means of reinforcing the structures that keep them in power. Similarly, we should be wary of anyone whose immediate reaction to a difficult circumstance is to accuse someone else of displeasing God or who demands that you shoulder burdens that are not yours to carry. We do not have to accept someone else's verdict on our lives when we are ultimately answerable only to God; we just have to remember that we *are* answerable to God for the weight on our own conscience.

There is another angle to consider regarding Job's companions, which is even more damning than their self-righteous sermons aimed at their suffering friend. The word traditionally translated as "Satan" throughout the Old Testament literally means "accuser" or "adversary" ("Satan" is a modified transliteration). The concept is often compared to that of a prosecuting attorney, which is quite apt for how we encounter the figure known as *satan* in the book of Job, as he answers to God in the heavenly courts. This is also, perhaps, why God rebukes Eliphaz, Bildad, and Zophar so severely in chapter 42, while excluding Elihu: the first three stood in the role of the accuser, repeatedly ordering Job to confess to sins he didn't commit, while Job pled his innocence. Eliphaz, Bildad, and Zophar firmly believed they were doing God's work as they browbeat Job on the hypothetical witness stand, invoking God's wrath and demanding confession, but they were actually acting as the accuser—as the *satan*.

May that stand as a warning to us all.

6

AMBIGUITY:
THE GOD OF THE INSCRUTABLE

> *Jonah 4*
> *Judges 4*
> *1 Samuel 14*
> *1 Samuel 25.2–42*

The story of Jonah is a story of one man up against the inscrutable. Jonah runs in the opposite direction when faced with incomprehensible orders to preach repentance to the warlord king of Assyria. He is a prophet raised to believe in a God of justice—a God who claims vengeance upon the enemies of God's people. Now, Jonah is tasked with offering those same enemies mercy. It's inconsistent with the God the prophet thinks he knows.

While Jonah's legacy is, unquestionably, dominated by his run-in with a large aquatic creature with a tendency to swallow its food whole, his story doesn't end in a pile of fish vomit on the beach, from whence he obediently makes his way to Nineveh. After finally completing his assignment after a few notable detours, Jonah retreats outside the city gates to see what will come of his reluctant evangelism. As he waits, he is teased with only temporary relief from the scorching desert sun as a leafy plant springs up to provide him shade; but a divinely appointed worm devours it overnight, leaving Jonah exposed once again as God stirs up "a sultry east wind" in the morning (4:8). The apparently inconsistent and unpredictable actions of God toward a supposedly beloved prophet leave Jonah confounded and furious: "But God said to Jonah, 'Is it right for you to be angry about the bush?' And he said, 'Yes, angry enough to die'" (Jon. 4:9). While Jonah is hardly a model of broad-mindedness and acceptance, he is nevertheless admirable in his honesty. He offers an elegant prayer of lament from the belly of the fish but doesn't couch his day-to-day dialogue with God in flowery speech or poetic pontifications. He doesn't try to pretend that he is a patient and loving man; instead, he announces to God in no uncertain terms that he is angry at the turn of events. Jonah may be many things, but he is no hypocrite.

With a short, two-verse lecture on Jonah's selfish callousness toward the people of Nineveh, the book concludes. We don't know how Jonah's story wraps up, and we don't know if he ever came to accept God's reasoning. In this way, the ending of the book reflects one of its primary themes: that God's ways are often inscrutable, confusing, and ostensibly illogical, and we may never be given a reason why. Whether you read the book as historical record or holy parody of the more traditional prophets, the story of Jonah speaks to the experience many of us have with God. It can feel as if we are trapped in a story we didn't choose and can't escape, with rules we don't understand and moral lessons that seem to run counter to the culture in which we've been raised.

In fact, the desire to create order out of a seemingly chaotic human existence is a near-universal response to confusion or uncertainty. When we struggle to grasp the *hows*, *whys*, and *whats* of life, a common solution is to create rules, assign clear-cut designations of right and wrong, and otherwise attempt to assert some form of predictability and control over the unknowable. Certainty gives us security in "rightness"; we understand our place when we see the world in black and white, us and them, right and wrong. But ambiguity in God's actions can lead to a destabilization of our worldview, our comfort, and our very identity. It can also lead to inaction, emotional paralysis, or bitterness.

Many of us can recount at least one cautionary sermon we've heard from the pulpit about King Saul's punishment for his premature sacrifice ahead of the prophet Samuel's arrival at Gilgal in 1 Samuel 13. When Samuel doesn't show up within seven days and the soldiers begin deserting, Saul takes it upon himself to perform the ritual of the burnt offerings to God ahead of the impending battle, even though this job unequivocally belongs to Samuel. When the prophet finally does arrive and learns of Saul's actions, he tells the king, "You have done foolishly; you have not kept the commandment of the LORD your God, which he commanded you. The LORD would have established your kingdom over Israel forever, but now your kingdom will not continue; the LORD has sought out a man after his own heart; and the LORD has appointed him to be ruler over his people, because you have not kept what the LORD commanded you" (13:13-14).

Similarly we can all likely recall 2 Samuel 6 and 1 Chronicles 13, when Uzzah dies reaching out to stop the ark of the covenant from falling while David, the successor prophesied about in the previous story, is transporting the ark in a celebratory procession to Jerusalem. God said not to touch the ark, Uzzah touches it, and he is killed on the spot. End of story. For those preachers willing to be a little more generous with their interpretations, perhaps God's anger was stirred because the people were transporting the ark by oxcart rather than in the way he instructed them by using carrying poles. But either way, Uzzah tries to help and God strikes him down.

These are harsh stories that are sometimes hard to accept for readers who are more comfortable with a little more gray, a little more leeway, a little more grace. It wasn't Saul's fault Samuel didn't show up on time. And wasn't Uzzah trying to do something good when he reached out? Likely it was just a reflexive response to seeing the ark of the covenant start to fall, and he wanted to

keep the sacred object from crashing to the ground. But the outcome in both cases is undeniable; it's spelled out clearly right
there in the text. And the lesson we should take from these stories,
we are so often told, is that God's commands are to be followed
to the strictest letter, even when we don't fully understand why.
Otherwise, the result is death—spiritually if not physically.

These stories are the perfect textual supports for a theology
rooted in legalism. Yes, they are part of the biblical text and therefore should be considered as part of the broader understanding
of the divine narrative of humanity, but the problem with stories
like these, and many others, is that they are often weaponized,
locking believers into a kind of spiritual guessing game as they
frantically try to discern God's will while fearing that one false
move will throw off God's plan for their entire lives or bring divine wrath down upon them. It is as if God is the talisman in the
classic horror story "The Monkey's Paw," by W. W. Jacobs, where
the mummified hand of a monkey grants wishes, but with violent
and terrible consequences for tampering with fate.

When other believers or church leaders try to silence anyone
who questions a narrow interpretation or censure people with
healthy boundaries, this is more than legalism—it is classic gaslighting. It is using power to imprison people into a life of holy
terror where one false move could spell their doom, or else it's an
attempt to convince people that what they know to be wrong is
somehow excusable or even condoned by God. And it is nothing
short of spiritual abuse.

Consider Beth's story. She grew up a preacher's kid in rural up-
state New York, in a church that emphasized traditional gender
roles as the be-all-and-end-all for marriage. Her first marriage
dissolved on the grounds of financial infidelity and abandonment, when her husband repeatedly emptied their bank accounts
and secretly opened credit cards in her name that he proceeded to
max out, meanwhile leaving her alone—sometimes for weeks at
a time—to face an empty pantry and possible eviction. When she

ended the marriage, her parents were so upset that they required that she stand before the congregation and "confess her sin" of divorce. Eventually, Beth met her second husband at church, and the couple moved to southern Florida for his job not long after their wedding. Beth began graduate school while working part time, but when the recession of 2008 impacted her husband's construction business, his behavior became increasingly erratic as his mental health declined:

> I tried to be the perfect Christian wife. I tried to do everything that the church people around me and the Bible said I was supposed to do. He was convinced I was cheating because I started wearing mascara and bought a few thongs because I'd been told we needed to have more sex.
>
> I was teaching at a school affiliated with my church and spent all day surrounded by old Christian ladies, but [my husband] was still convinced I was having an affair at work. He became abusive. He took my phone, locked me inside, pulled me by my hair, raped me. I tried to talk to the elders at my church, but they said things like "Eve was made for Adam, so you cannot refuse or deny him anything." They told me there was no such thing as marital rape. Every time I went to talk with them, they always asked what I was doing to submit. The answer was always the same: put him first, be more submissive, have more sex, pray more. My parents said the same thing. At night I would sit on the other side of the locked door while my husband pounded on it and screamed at me that he was going to tear it down, and I wondered what about this scenario was me not doing enough. Was "submitting" letting him hit me? I was praying constantly for God to help me, but there was never any change. I was financially dependent on [my spouse], so I couldn't afford a place on my own, and my parents were still so convinced I was such a sinner because of my failed first marriage that they had largely cut ties. . . .

I felt totally abandoned by God and totally betrayed by the church and by my faith. They were so stuck in their simple an-swers that they couldn't see past the legalistic point that since he technically hadn't cheated on me, I had no grounds to leave him, even though he was so violent I was afraid he was going to kill me. It was like my divorce somehow reflected poorly on them. Since the school was associated with my church, I wor-ried that even if I did divorce him, I would be out of a job if they felt it wasn't "scriptural." . . . Sure enough, when I finally escaped with the help of the former principal of the school, I did lose my job. . . .

Finally, after almost a decade of no contact, my parents reached out to me to apologize. They had truly believed they were being good parents, but they finally saw how horrific they were to treat their own daughter, or anyone, that way in the name of Jesus.

Legalism is, ultimately, a form of control. It is an attempt to control the behavior of other people by restricting their choices or causing them to live in fear of making a wrong move, and it is also an attempt to control God by forcing God into a position of acknowledging or finding pleasure in the extra effort. As Beth experienced, the Christian institutions in her life placed the let-ter of the law above her physical safety, forcing her to bear the burden of someone else's desire to appear holy. It is legalism at its most insidious.

In 1 Samuel 14, we encounter a less-often-preached-on story about Saul, this one involving his son Jonathan and some fateful honey. Following a strenuous battle against the Philistines that resulted in a major victory for the Israelite army, the weary sol-diers stumble into the forest to rest. There they find a honeycomb so full that it is spilling over onto the ground; nevertheless, no one takes a single taste, since "Saul committed a very rash act on that day. He had laid an oath on the troops, saying, 'Cursed be anyone who eats food before it is evening and I have been avenged on my enemies'" (14:24). Jonathan, however, had not been present when his father made the pronouncement, so he tastes the honey and is immediately reinvigorated. After he is informed of his violation of the oath, he scoffs, saying: "My father has troubled the land; see how my eyes have brightened because I tasted a little of this honey. How much better if today the troops had eaten freely of the spoil taken from their enemies; for now the slaughter among the Philistines has not been great" (14:29-30).

The Israelites see the sense of Jonathan's words, and fall to feasting on the plunder of the battle; unfortunately, in their famished state, they do not wait to properly drain the meat of blood, causing Saul to declare them to be acting treacherously, since Leviticus 17:14 strictly forbids consuming the blood of an animal.

Let's pause to consider the role of legalism in this story so far. First, "Saul committed a very rash act"—that is, he was steered by his own desires and ego rather than consultation with God. Secondly, "He had laid an oath on the troops," forbidding them from taking the sustenance they needed. This one Scripture (14:24) strikes at the very heart of legalism: it demands extra measures that God does not require, and then it takes one person's issues and places them on the backs of others.

The result is a classic act of rebellion. As soon as they realize how ludicrous their situation really is, the men throw all caution to the wind and behave in a way that they know is a violation of their religious laws. And Saul's reaction is, again, textbook legalism. When word of the soldiers' actions reaches Saul, he announces:

> "You have dealt treacherously; roll a large stone before me here." Saul said, "Disperse yourselves among the troops, and say to them, 'Let all bring their oxen or their sheep, and slaughter them here, and eat; and do not sin against the LORD by eating with the blood.'" So all of the troops brought their oxen

with them that night, and slaughtered them there. And Saul
built an altar to the LORD; it was the first altar that he built to
the LORD. (14:33-35)

Pay attention to Saul's choice of words: "You have dealt
treacherously." Nowhere does he acknowledge his own guilt for
putting burdensome and unhealthy restrictions on his men; he
is, however, quick to point out *their* guilt. Notice, too, the highly
significant detail included in verse 35; the altar Saul assembled
requiring his men to atone for consuming blood "was the first
altar that he built to the LORD." Never before had Saul erected a
stone of sacrifice on behalf of his own sins, but he was very eager
to put one up to correct the behavior of someone else.

But the story doesn't stop there. Saul wants to resume the battle immediately and fight the Philistines through the night, and
his advisors have no qualms; the priest, however, suggests, "Let
us draw near to God here," and so Saul inquires of God whether
his plan will succeed. He receives only silence in response, for
God "did not answer him that day" (14:36-37). Saul immediately
begins to rant, swearing that he will root out that cause of God's
displeasure, declaring: "Even if it is in my son Jonathan, he shall
surely die!" (14:39). He begins casting lots to determine guilt, but
"the people were cleared" (14:41), so Saul then swears on his son's
life again and casts a final lot, and it falls to Jonathan. He demands
an accounting, and Jonathan answers honestly:

> "I tasted a little honey with the tip of the staff that was in my
> hand; here I am, I will die." Saul said, "God do so to me and
> more also; you shall surely die, Jonathan!" Then the people said
> to Saul, "Shall Jonathan die, who has accomplished this great
> victory in Israel? Far from it! As the LORD lives, not one hair of
> his head shall fall to the ground; for he has worked with God
> today." So the people ransomed Jonathan, and he did not die.
> Then Saul withdrew from pursuing the Philistines; and the Phi-
> listines went to their own place. (14:43-46)

Once again, we see Saul's legalism at work even as God uses the lots to unmask the king's true nature. Throughout the process, Saul continues to protest his own innocence while repeatedly calling down condemnation on someone else. Jonathan confesses to the violation of his father's rash oath, and Saul is so intent on winning God's favor with his outrageous promises that he completely misses the fact that the rest of the Israelite army sees plainly: Jonathan "has worked with God today" (14:44). Thankfully, the levelheaded response of the people ultimately frees Jonathan from Saul's reckless posturing. Unlike many legalists, though, it seems Saul had the capacity to recognize his own foolishness when it was laid out before him in plain terms—at least this time.

It's no wonder that legalism was one of the primary religious practices Jesus spoke against in his teaching. Interestingly, however, Jesus also put extra restrictions on his followers when he preached sermons like the Beatitudes; or when he made sweeping pronouncements such as "You have heard that it was said to those of ancient times, 'You shall not murder'; and 'whoever murders shall be liable to judgment.' But I say to you that if you are angry with a brother or sister, you will be liable to judgment; and if you insult a brother or sister, you will be liable to the council; and if you say, 'You fool,' you will be liable to the hell of fire" (Matt. 5:21-22) and "You have heard that it was said, 'You shall not commit adultery.' But I say to you that everyone who looks at a woman with lust has already committed adultery with her in her heart" (Matt. 5:27-28). But there is one key difference between the additional burdens of Jesus and those of the Pharisees and Sadducees: When Jesus expanded the definitions of the sins, *it was always to protect the other person rather than to elevate the individual.* He sought to keep people from carrying grudges that could lead to violence. He sought

He was telling his followers to take the weight of forgiveness, self-control, temperance, fidelity, and love upon themselves, not to pass the burden on to other people.

to honor women by acknowledging that men were responsible for their own lustful thoughts. He honored women again when he restricted the acceptable reasons for divorce, by limiting the grounds for which their husbands could demand a dissolution of the marriage to just adultery; the expansion of the definition was not intended to shackle people to an unsafe situation, as we read about above in Beth's story, but to protect women from being cast out for any and every reason, thus leaving them without a means of shelter or protection in a fiercely patriarchal society (5:31-32). Jesus encouraged people to focus less on the dramatic conditions of their oaths and more on their reliability and trustworthiness in keeping them (5:33-37). He even encouraged his followers not to love only their neighbors, but to love all people (5:43-44). Jesus's expansion of the law beyond the text was not about elevating one's own self, but about elevating other people. He was telling his followers to take the weight of forgiveness, self-control, temperance, fidelity, and love upon themselves, not to pass the burden on to other people.

Yet despite Jesus's best efforts to break down structures of religious power concentrated in legalistic interpretations of "rightness," many today still struggle with the moral restraints put upon us by our faith traditions or even by ourselves. When God's will is ambiguous, the concreteness of rules can offer comfort. And if some rules are good, more must be better, right? So we begin down the path of creating more and more restrictions or regulations about what must be done or not done and how it must be done or not done. Because we don't have clear answers from God to dictate each step, we may worry that we, too, will suffer Uzzah's fate by acting impetuously and inadvertently offending God in the process. And so, with the sincerest of motives and purest of intentions, we erect fences and establish laws where there are none. In this case, we run up against a kind of personal legalism.

In some cases, personal legalism can be a kind of self-aggrandizement, where an individual believes that they are somehow "extra holy" and therefore have a higher standard than the average believer—almost like an arrogant version of the additional biblically sanctioned purity laws applicable only to those descended from the priestly line of Aaron. But more often than not, this kind of struggle with extra restrictions is due to sincere humility and a genuine desire to please God.

Abby, a former preacher's wife, ran into exactly this kind of struggle as she dealt with the aftermath of the divorce from her husband, despite his multiple affairs:

> I found I had put extra restrictions on myself. Something I had decided way back when I was a teenager was that if I ever got divorced, I would never remarry. I didn't expect anyone else to have to live by this . . . but I felt that I would still be bound by my vows because those were promises I made before God, and my conscience said I needed to keep them. So that was just what I thought my life would be when I did end up getting divorced. But then [a few months after the divorce], I woke up in the middle of the night with the clearest sense of God saying to me, "You aren't bound by those vows anymore, because in the society where those biblical laws were written, he [the ex-husband] would have been stoned. You are now under the protection of widowhood." It wasn't like I heard the voice of God booming or anything, but I just had a strong sense of him telling me this and setting me free from this burden I had placed on myself.

As Abby discovered, the key to overcoming such self-imposed austere thinking is to focus on finding freedom and joy in God rather than anxiety, nervousness, or fear of condemnation over unintentional sin. Of course, that's easier said than done, but there are examples throughout Scripture.

In Luke 17, we see a story that runs counter to the rigid, prescriptive, and often terrifying stories where God looms like a malevolent fairy or vengeful genie in an old tale, just waiting to catch someone in a technicality. Although a short story, it contains multitudes:

On the way to Jerusalem Jesus was going through the region
between Samaria and Galilee. As he entered a village, ten lepers
approached him. Keeping their distance, they called out, saying, "Jesus, Master, have mercy on us!" When he saw them, he
said to them, "Go and show yourselves to the priests." And as
they went, they were made clean. Then one of them, when he
saw that he was healed, turned back, praising God with a loud
voice. He prostrated himself at Jesus' feet and thanked him.
And he was a Samaritan. Then Jesus asked, "Were not ten made
clean? But the other nine, where are they? Was none of them
found to return and give praise to God except this foreigner?"
Then he said to him, "Get up and go on your way; your faith has
made you well." (17:11–19)

The lepers did not even have to wait until they reached the religious authorities; their leprosy was healed en route. One man,
however, turned back as soon as he realized what had happened,
and returned to Jesus to thank him even before going to the
priests as Jesus had commanded. But rather than reafflicting the
disobedient person, Jesus praises the man's spontaneous act of
genuine worship, gratefulness, and celebration, and even asks
why the others did not return as well.

So, what is the lesson we should derive from this story? Is it that
the (now former) leper was "adding to the word of God" by returning? After all, he technically is not following the command of Jesus
to the letter. Or should we take an example from his pure impulse
of praise to engage with God in the most honest way we can?

Interestingly, the narrative takes pains to point out twice that
this lone man who broke ranks was not an Israelite. First, the
text notes, "And he was a Samaritan" (17:16), and second, Jesus
asks why no one else returned to "give praise to God except this
foreigner" (17:18). The Samaritans were a Semitic people from
the northern tribes but separated from the main body of Israel

between the fourth and third centuries BCE, recognizing themselves as both ethnically and religiously distinct, despite still adhering to monotheistic worship of YHWH. One of the greatest differences between the Samaritans and the Jews is that the Samaritans hold only the first five books of the Jewish Old Testament as sacred and specifically reject any teachings about King David in large part because he moved the Jewish capital from Shechem, which is located in Samaria, to Jerusalem. In other words, this "foreigner" would not have been taught the cautionary tale of Uzzah in either 2 Samuel or 1 Chronicles. Of course, it is only conjecture, but perhaps this man was the sole person to break ranks because he did not carry the same cultural baggage as the others. He didn't reject a legalistic interpretation of Jesus's instructions from a desire to cut corners or "get away with something." He acted from his natural impulse to show appreciation, to praise God, and to acknowledge the kindness of Jesus, and he was honored for his grateful disobedience.

Marco, a teacher in his thirties, describes his own struggle with cultural baggage:

> I come from a family that ended every sentence with "Lord willing." It was like I couldn't make a single decision without first analyzing the situation from every possible angle. I don't mean just that I'm a planner and I like to think things through, but I felt trapped, like I had to imagine every single angle before I could make a decision. You know how they say that Hamlet had "analysis paralysis," because every time he has to make a decision in the play he goes into some long soliloquy and talks himself out of whatever he was about to do? That was how I felt, like I had to dissect every single thing to figure out if I might possibly make God mad with a choice, even if I knew in my gut that it was the right thing to do. I got locked in a bunch of "what ifs?" and ended up not doing a lot of things I knew

I should actually be doing because, if I looked hard enough, I could always find a reason why God might have a problem with it, and then I'd be outside God's will. . . . I always thought about the story of Gideon and the wool [Judg. 6:36–40], when Gideon kept asking God for different signs so he could be sure of his will. I would do the same thing until I was sure he was giving me clear directions or I could at least convince myself that's what the signs were saying. The problem is that God really doesn't work that way.

The question that Marco struggled with, as do many of us, is when is taking matters into our own hands disobeying God and when is it divinely inspired action? Oftentimes, people will point to Genesis 16, when Abraham and Sarah used the maidservant Hagar as a surrogate, as an example of the problems that can come from not "waiting on the Lord." As we will see in chapter 7, the initial promise was only that the child would be descended from Abraham; Sarah was not mentioned in the first promise. Abraham was told he would sire a child, but Sarah was postmenopausal, so they found another way to make it happen that followed a common custom of their culture (however problematic it was regarding issues of ownership and consent).[1] True, the result was tremendous discord within the family and two warring nations—but nowhere does the text tell us that Ishmael should never have been born or that he was not part of God's design. In fact, God actually goes to special pains to preserve Ishmael's life in Genesis 21. So, when do our prayers and actions set us in right relationship with the Lord, and when do they set us up for disaster?

Unfortunately, as Marco pointed out, during periods of particularly strong contention with God, we may view inaction as our only option as we "wait for the LORD" (Isa. 40:31) out of fear or deference for his will. But such terrified inaction is hardly the "life in abundance" we are promised in John 10. Life demands decisions, and just as there are many examples of people who were tripped up by technicalities or who paid a steep price for acting of their own accord, there are also many examples of people who did not agonize over their bold steps that undermined the sacred structures ruling their society. Free from the fear that legalism uses to control and constrain, these individuals acted with swift assurance and confidence in God's blessing upon their unflinching choices.

In Judges 4, we encounter a story that celebrates bold action at every turn. When Deborah, the presiding judge of Israel, summons Barak of the tribe of Naphtali to come before her, she declares him selected by the Lord to lead the Israelite armies against Sisera, a Canaanite general. After Deborah describes the battle plan in which God expressly promises to deliver the enemy directly to him for defeat, Barak nevertheless responds reluctantly, accepting his divine charge only conditionally, telling Deborah: "'If you will go with me, I will go; but if you will not go with me, I will not go.' And she said, 'I will surely go with you; nevertheless, the road on which you are going will not lead to your glory, for the LORD will sell Sisera into the hand of a woman'" (4:8-9). For his hesitation, Barak is chastised. Because he prioritized hedging his bets rather than moving decisively, "the road" on which he was going was not marked by the fullness of honor that should have been his. The victory is not stripped from the Israelites, but it is removed from Barak.

Instead, that glory goes to Jael, the wife of a prominent Kenite named Heber. Their tribe maintained a kind of liminal status—both friendly with the Canaanites and distantly related to the Israelites through Moses's father-in-law—but Heber had struck an agreement with the local Canaanite king, so Jael and Heber lived apart from the rest of the Kenites. Because of this alliance, as Sisera fled from the battlefield, he sought shelter in Jael's tent, where she served him milk, covered him with a thick rug, and waited for him to fall asleep before driving an iron tent peg through his temple with a hammer, pinning his head to the ground. For her boldness, Jael is praised as "Most blessed of women" by Deborah (Judg. 5:24).

This story may surprise a modern audience for its violence, but it would have shocked an ancient readership for an altogether different reason: Jael clearly violated the cultural rules of hospitality, commonly known now by the Greek name *xenia*. The basic tenets of *xenia* were generally consistent throughout the ancient Near East and Mediterranean; they maintained that strangers were to be welcomed, and as long as they remained guests in the household, they were considered under the protection of the host and no harm was to come to them. This accounts for the explicit commands regarding the proper treatment of strangers in passages like Leviticus 19:33-34, Deuteronomy 10:19, Ezekiel 47:22, and elsewhere. It also accounts for Abraham's eager hospitality to the angels who frequented his tent, as well as the anger of God against the city of Sodom in the highly problematic story in Genesis 19. When the men of the city demand that Lot hand over the angels in the form of visitors who are staying in his home, the residents of Sodom are violating the sacred practice of *xenia*, and they are struck blind for their actions (19:11).

A small detail in Judges 4:19 makes clear that Jael offered Sisera every reason to believe he was being welcomed in the spirit of *xenia*. When he asks her for water, she goes above and beyond and serves him milk. The significance of this act is noted again in Deborah's song of praise in the following chapter, when she observes:

> "He asked water and she gave him milk,
>   she brought him curds in a lordly bowl." (5:25)

Sisera interprets the gesture as it was intended, to indicate that he was an honored guest who would be treated as family, and he immediately asks Jael to stand guard at the door of the tent. Clearly, he expects that he will be afforded the protection of her household.

Rather than wringing her hands over whether she might bring down the anger of God upon herself for committing the cultural and scriptural taboo of acting in violence against someone who has taken sanctuary within her household under the auspices of *xenia*, Jael sees what needs to be done and she acts. It seems rather significant that the author of Judges, a book concerned with the history of legal order in Israel, should celebrate Jael's transgression of both the custom and the law ("Thou shalt not kill"), without hesitation—and yet, there she is, the hero of the story praised in the narrative as well as in song. It is the glory that would have belonged to Barak had he not hemmed and hawed.

The story of Abigail in 1 Samuel 25 is another shining example of a person who acted swiftly and wisely as the situation required, rather than rendering herself incapacitated by technicalities and expectations. David, while in the wilderness of Paran, sends an envoy of men to appeal to a wealthy herder named Nabal, husband of the wise and beautiful Abigail. The men appeal to Nabal's hospitality for the king and his troops, reminding him of the protection and respect they had recently offered his men and his flocks. But Nabal, who is described in the text as being evil and "surly and mean," rudely turns away David's emissaries with shouting and insults (25:3).

The king, of course, is furious when he learns of this slight. In true David fashion, he drastically overreacts and prepares four hundred men to charge Nabal's camp with the intention of killing every single male member of the household, but one of Nabal's servants informs Abigail of everything that occurred. Abigail does not pause to ponder what a submissive wife ought to do; instead, she hurries to prepare a lavish feast and sets out to meet David but does not tell her husband (25:18-19). When she finally sees the king, she prostrates herself before him and cries, "My lord, do not take seriously this ill-natured fellow, Nabal; for as his name is, so is he; Nabal [fool] is his name, and folly is with him" (25:25). She then hastens to praise David and reason with him that such a drastic response is unwarranted and that she hopes, at the end of his life, he "shall have no cause of grief, or pangs of conscience, for having shed blood without cause" (25:31).

And what is David's reaction to this woman who would so blatantly and shamelessly defy her husband as well as talk down a recklessly impetuous king?

"Blessed be the LORD, the God of Israel, who sent you to meet me today!" he announces. "Blessed be your good sense, and blessed be you, who have kept me today from bloodguilt and from avenging myself by my own hand!" (25:32-33).

Not "blessed be your obedience" or "blessed be your submission." No, the man after God's own heart declares, "Blessed be your good sense." Abigail acted swiftly according to her wisdom and intuition rather than agonizing over an obstinate adherence to the law or cultural inhibitions placed on her behavior, and she was blessed for it.

In Luke 5 and Mark 2, we encounter another example of unapologetic action in the story of the man with paralysis whose friends carried him on a mat to be healed by Jesus, "but finding no way to bring him in because of the crowd, they went up on the roof and let him down with his bed through the tiles into the middle of the crowd in front of Jesus" (Luke 5:19). They do not act timidly, nor do they apologize for their actions—not just jumping the line or cutting a hole in someone's roof, but also of dropping a person right in Jesus's face. The friends saw what needed to be done, they recognized what resources were within their power, they took action accordingly, and Jesus responded.

Sometimes, it can feel as if our desire to be a faithful Christian has killed our sense of intuition instead of allowing us to trust the Holy Spirit to guide us where there are no clear answers. When we are raised in a culture that seems to delight in drawing legalistic conclusions from ambiguous stories or mining the Bible for cautionary tales to keep us locked into a rigid set of behaviors (some of which even go against the spirit of Christ's teachings), we can become denigrated to the point that we no longer feel worth or confidence in our own decisions. When we fear to act because we might unwittingly step outside the right/wrong dichotomy we have been told dictates the universe, we become bumbling fools rather than perpetually growing and maturing beings made in the very image of God.

We don't know exactly why Uzzah was struck down. We don't know what God's ultimate plan was for Jonah and Ishmael. And here's the kicker—*our salvation does not depend on us figuring those things out.* God's ambiguity does not preclude us from action. The point of the Christian life is not to be right at every turn; it is to grow in relationship with God and with the people around us. When we demand perfection from ourselves and from everyone else, we will always be trapped in a farce of morality: Whose definition of "perfection"? Whose basis for evaluation? Whose measure of morality? But more than that, we are denying the role of grace. We are called to life, which sometimes means making choices and taking action even without clear direction. The most any of us can do is to make the best decision we can in the moment rather than allowing ourselves to be frozen in indecision and legalistic fear. We may miss the opportunity to do good when we are obsessed with the pursuit of being right.

> *The point of the Christian life is not to be right at every turn; it is to grow in relationship with God and with the people around us.*

As his book closes, Jonah is still pouting outside of Nineveh, far more upset about the loss of the plant that kept him comfortable than about the impending fate of the thousands of lives inside the city walls. There is no resolution offered, no further exposition, no glimpse at what happens to the city and the people, no redeeming character arc for Jonah to leave the experience a changed man. The book simply . . . ends. Perhaps Jonah's story offers no satisfying finale because there is no place to go when we are stuck in the mindset of legalism. There is no further work God can do with us, no further growth or purpose or development for which we are fit if we are so stuck in our "rightness" that we miss the humanity in front of us.

7

ABANDONMENT:
THE GOD WHO NO LONGER FEELS PRESENT

Genesis 17
2 Chronicles 32:27–31
John 11:1–44

More than one hundred verses assure us, in one form or another, that God will never leave or forsake God's people—and yet it is almost inevitable that we will all feel an acute sense of abandonment at some point in our lives. We believe that if we just had more faith, sinned less, prayed harder, gave more freely, we would feel God's constant presence with us; after all, James 4:8 promises, "Draw near to God, and he will draw near to you." But sometimes, no amount of fasting or prayer or confession or purification can turn a situation around. We beg God to let us know we are not alone, and we are answered with . . . crickets.

King David struggled with these feelings throughout his life. His heart-wrenching verses in the lament psalms, where he compares his emotional state to a miserable pit, are surprisingly empathetic to the state in which many people find themselves in the midst of ongoing struggles. In Psalm 13, he cries out:

How long, O LORD? Will you forget me forever?
　　How long will you hide your face from me?
How long must I bear pain in my soul,
　　and have sorrow in my heart all day long?
How long shall my enemy be exalted over me? (13:1–2)

He expresses a similar sentiment in Psalm 42:

I say to God, my rock,
　　"Why have you forgotten me?
Why must I walk about mournfully
　　because the enemy oppresses me?"
As with a deadly wound in my body,
　　my adversaries taunt me,
while they say to me continually,
　　"Where is your God?" (42:9–10)

In fact, the book of Psalms contains roughly thirty individual laments and a dozen more communal ones.

One interesting passage in Psalm 138 reads,

The LORD will vindicate me;
　　your love, LORD, endures forever—
　　do not abandon the works of your hands.
　　(138:8 NIV)

At first glance, the verse seems to be a reassurance: God will be triumphant in the end. We can have full confidence in the Lord; it says so right here in the text! But the sentence ends with a plea: "Do not abandon the works of your hands." It is almost as if the writer is trying to convince himself of the first half of the statement: "God will see this through according to his will, right? You won't forget me, God, . . . will you?" That's not quite as comforting. For a "man after God's own heart," David certainly seems to have felt abandoned a lot.

◦ ◦ ◦

What do we do when we have fasted and prayed for God to let us feel the divine presence and yet are met with resounding silence? How do we respond when people tell us, "If God seems distant, who do you think moved?" What do we do with promises, like Jeremiah 33:3 ("Call to me and I will answer you"), that can sometimes feel as if they are mocking us in our pain?

Many of us have been assured by well-meaning comforters that God would never, ever leave us alone, and yet, interestingly, the Bible gives us several examples of God physically withdrawing from faithful servants for a period of time. The first instance is in Genesis 17, when God establishes the covenant of circumcision, changes the names of the patriarch and matriarch Abram and Sarai to Abraham and Sarah, and clarifies the earlier assurance regarding Abraham's heir. Previously, the promise had been offered only to Abraham, with no mention of his wife; he was simply told: "no one but your very own issue shall be your heir" (15:4). The child would come from Abraham's line, but no such promises are offered at the time to Sarah. It is not until thirteen years later and the problematic involvement of a slave woman as a surrogate that God explains further the rather far-fetched plan for the promised child to be born from Sarah's nonagenarian body.

The stories set up a scenario that will be mirrored more than forty generations later with the announcement of Jesus's birth under similarly unlikely circumstances, only this time it is a young, unmarried woman who will bear the promised son. In the Gospels, when the announcement is completed, Mary immediately conceives the Messiah—the long-awaited epiphany of God making his presence among humans. In Genesis, however, just the opposite occurs; rather than the Almighty dwelling among those chosen vessels, we are told, "And when he had finished talking with him, God went up from Abraham" (17:22). In other words, God left. The term translated "went up" can be translated in a number of ways, including in the sense of "rose up from," such as the sun at dawn (19:15) or rising smoke (19:28), or alter-

nately, "departed from," as when Abraham "went up from" Egypt
(13:1) or Lot left Zoar (19:30). The idea is that there is a movement away from the previous position; in this case, God removed
the divine presence from Abraham—albeit very temporarily, as
God appears again just a short time later at the opening of the
next chapter. Nevertheless, it is interesting that, of all the times
that God appeared to Abraham, only here are we told that God
also departed, and it comes on the heels of the most outrageous
promise—so outrageous, in fact, that Abraham laughs at the pronouncement (17:17), as does his wife when she hears a repetition
of the promise a few verses later (18:12). It seems that, perhaps,
when God "went up from" Abraham and Sarah, it was a stepping
back to test the faith of God's servants in the face of such laugh-
ably absurd circumstances.

If this reading of God's temporary removal seems too much of
a stretch from which to draw theological lessons, let us explore
another instance where the text specifically tells us that God
physically withdrew the divine presence. In 2 Chronicles 32, we
read about King Hezekiah, upon whom life seemed to smile: God
had given him "very great riches" (32:27), and, just in case that
wasn't enough, "Hezekiah prospered in all his works" (32:30).
And yet even Hezekiah, who seems to be the living epitome of
the #blessed stereotype, endured a period of abandonment. When
he is faced with a major meeting with an official envoy from Babylon—the most powerful, feared, and ruthless empire in the region—God does not give Hezekiah an extra measure of strength,
nor does God keep a hand steadfastly on Hezekiah during this
crucial and likely nerve-wracking meeting. Quite the opposite.
"God left him to himself, in order to test him and to know all that
was in his heart" (32:31). Here, the verb leaves no room for ambiguity. It is the same root word used in Psalm 22:1, "My God, my
God, why have you forsaken me?" which is, of course, the very
Scripture Jesus cried out from the cross. This was no stepping
briefly to the side; God withdrew entirely from Hezekiah.

So, what do we make of those well-intentioned reassurances that God never leaves us alone when it can certainly feel otherwise? How do we respond when those promises of presence sometimes seem empty? How do we know when we are being tested and when we are being rejected—especially when the two feel exactly the same? It's hard to reconcile the image of a loving God with one who leaves us alone to fall on our faces at times. It's not simply a parent letting go of the back of a child's bike with the training wheels removed—it's failing to move a muscle when the bike tips and the child hits the pavement. Is God really the kind parent who knows our every need—the one whose "eye is on the sparrow"? Or is God much more detached, like the supreme being of Deism, who created the world by setting things in motion and then stepped back and let things run their course?

Perhaps you've asked these same questions yourself and been met with resistance or even reprimand. For many believers brought up in the evangelical tradition, to believe in anything short of a God who is intimately invested in every detail of our daily lives is akin to rejecting the idea of God altogether. Rita, a stay-at-home mom in her fifties, explained her experience this way:

> I was in a discussion with some other believers a few years ago while I was going through an especially hard time. Nothing I did was working out, no matter how hard I tried to follow God's will. It felt a little like a slap in the face. But when I said that it felt like God had walked away from me, a couple of people immediately got offended, saying stuff like "You know better than that!" and "You're blaspheming the Holy Spirit by saying that because the Holy Spirit is God's promise that he will never leave us." Even when I tried to show examples from the Bible, it was like the idea was too different from their picture of God so they wouldn't consider it. I think maybe it scared them too much to think about it. They just kept telling me over and over

that they thought my faith was stronger than that. So now I was being judged for my feelings instead of being helped through my bad times.

The issue Rita faced in her small group, and that many of us may identify with, was not that her understanding of God might need a little recalibration, but that there was something wrong with her for feeling that way. This is classic deflection, a manipulative technique where the topic of conversation is redirected ever so slightly from the issue at hand to the person making the complaint. It takes the blame from the offending party and places it on the victim. In Rita's case, rather than acknowledging the struggle, mystery, and apparent disconnect between biblical promises and her own experiences, it was easier for the Christians around her to shift the focus to Rita herself. The entire conversation switched from helping her through her spiritual struggles to identifying and addressing a problem the other believers insisted was inherent *in her person*. Her honest questions were regarded as tantamount to a character flaw. This is a favorite technique of denominational apologists who are unwilling to entertain any questions that go against the theology they teach or that might threaten their own comfortable understandings of God—and it is classic gaslighting.

But if Jesus, in his moment of deepest despair, felt compelled to ask, "Why have you forsaken me?" surely we are allowed to do the same without censure.

Sometimes there are no easy answers—or even hard ones. Sometimes it is impossible to know what is going on behind the scenes in God's greater plan. Sometimes our entire understanding of faith and relationship with God may be turned on its head. But if Jesus, in his moment of deepest despair, felt compelled to ask, "Why have you forsaken me?" surely we are allowed to do the same without censure.

Even if we cannot solve the enduring mystery of *why*, maybe we can find answers in the question of *how*. If our old notions of

God have left us feeling abandoned, perhaps we can look around us and see if God is simply present in another form. God is, after all, quite good at showing up in unexpected ways: as a burning bush, as a column of cloud or fire, as a whirlwind, as a wrestling man, as a dove, as a poor baby in a manger . . .

Maybe the better question to ask ourselves is *how* we reengage with God after our entire world has been rocked to its very foundation—when our entire life has been changed in an instant and there is no going back to the way things were before. This is the reality many of us faced in 2020 as the COVID-19 pandemic swept the globe. Within a matter of weeks, our society was shut down and life as we knew it came to a screeching halt. Churches and schools scrambled to develop an online presence to meet spiritual and educational needs. Businesses that had taken years to establish were shuttered while hospitals struggled to provide care for all the patients coming in. Where was God in the midst of all that suffering? How could the Creator of the universe seemingly turn away from the entire human race just at a time when we needed God most? How many people around the world were praying for deliverance with no divine intervention forthcoming?

And yet, God did show up. God showed up in neighbors bringing each other meals. God showed up in the hearts of people who were willing to wear masks and avoid nursing homes and other care facilities in order to offer an extra barrier of protection to the most vulnerable populations. God showed up in science, as researchers rushed to develop a vaccine. God does not always show up in dramatic God-form; more often than not, the Lord makes the divine presence known through small stirrings of compassion in someone's heart or acts of love toward another part of God's creation.

Of course, this can all sound very Pollyannaish when you're suddenly faced with eviction and no one volunteers to take you in until you can get on your feet. Or when you desperately need a friend but only feel rejection. Or when you have spent months praying for a job but no one will give you a chance. Sometimes there simply are no answers. There is no satisfactory reason anyone can offer as to why God doesn't seem to have shown up. It can threaten a person's sense of spiritual security to say, "I don't know what God is doing here" or "The Bible really doesn't offer us a good explanation except that God's absences never seem to be permanent." For some people, the mere acknowledgment that there are some spiritual issues for which there are no answers is deeply unsettling. And yet, there are some questions that defy our understanding and some traumas that cut too deeply to be cured with words.

Noah understood the burden all too well. His entire way of life was wiped out in the most literal sense, and nothing looked the same after he stepped off the ark. How do you rebuild your life after a tragedy of that magnitude? How do you rebuild *the world*? What do we do when the whole way that we understood the universe suddenly shifts—and the God we thought we knew no longer looks the same? How do we adjust when our old notion of God has left us forever and we must either adopt a whole new concept of the divine or else leave the void unfilled?

After leaving the ark, the first nonreligious act that the Bible describes Noah engaging in is planting a vineyard and subsequently getting drunk (Gen. 9:20). It is a series of events that sheds a bit of light on Noah's character. First, we see him coaxing life out of the ruined earth as he actively cultivates a plant. He is described as "a man of the soil"—the same descriptor used throughout Genesis 2 to narrate how God formed all living things, including Adam, out of the dust of the earth. This vineyard is, in a very real way, the creation moment of a new earth.

Only, a truly blank slate isn't really possible, because even in a new beginning, memories of the old traumas remain. To apply a modern lens to the text, Noah's drunkenness may even be interpreted as a symptom of PTSD as he struggles to cope with the survivor's guilt of being among the only ones chosen to survive.

This pattern repeats itself in Genesis 19, when Lot shelters in a cave with his daughters following the destruction of Sodom and Gomorrah. Convinced that they are the last living souls on earth, his daughters ply him with wine in order to impregnate themselves with the intention of keeping the command to be fruitful and multiply that God gave at both the original creation and the reboot (Gen. 19:30–35). They succeed in making Lot so drunk that he is completely oblivious to their presence. Again, reading this deeply troubling passage

> *A truly blank slate isn't really possible, because even in a new beginning, memories of the old traumas remain.*

through a modern lens, it is not unreasonable to wonder whether Lot's willingness to consume so much alcohol was not, at least in part, an effort to escape the memories and guilt of the catastrophe he just experienced. Noah plants a vineyard. Lot sires children. The spark of the divine is present in the miracle of new growth; perhaps scraping a bit of life out of destruction is one way to rediscover God.

Joe, a military veteran, shares the feelings of abandonment he experienced following his return from his fifth overseas deployment in March 2010. Everything about the faith he had been brought up with seemed to have shattered. "It felt like God went out for a pack of cigarettes and didn't come back," he explained as he struggled to readjust to life at home.

> I had a lot of friends in combat, and so many were getting killed on convoys and things like that. . . . We were part of the big push into Marjah [Afghanistan] just as tensions were escalating, and then when I got home I had orders to the Gulf Coast, which had always been the beaches I visited as a kid. But the Deep Water Horizon oil spill happened at the same time, only four weeks after I got back to the States.
> There had been destruction of the natural world where I found solace; the place I was most looking forward to going

when I got back to normal life had just been tar-balled and destroyed, and I had been really sick and hidden an ongoing autoimmune condition just to be medically cleared to go on that deployment. Now not only had I lost a sense of innocence and lost a sense of perspective, and trust in the institution I was serving . . . I felt like what I wanted and needed, and what I was able to take responsibility for and understand, were not the same thing. The way that my faith had been taught to me, and what I thought I was supposed to do, didn't make me feel better. And even hearing that sounds a little spoiled. A lot of evangelicalism is like a franchise: "If you do this, your life will be better. You can avoid problems!"

I would ask myself, "Am I doing it wrong? I don't think so. But what works? Because it's clearly not this."

Much like Noah, Joe sought to coax life out of the ground. Prior to his last deployment, he'd planned to start a garden, and now he took up the idea once again as a way to find his way back to life.

It was almost like I was trying to turn back the clock. I bought a rototiller and soil, and started doing research and planted this hedge of blueberries. I heard an old lady at a nursery say once, "You really can bury a lot of your problems in the soil; or at least, you think you can." I did European-style drinking, where I would have just enough to keep me slightly buzzed all day. I would go outside in a state of reduced awareness so that I could allow my brain to be fully consumed with what I was doing.

This blueberry thing was one of the greatest business failures of all time. I did the math at some point and I think it was close to $1,500 a quart. But for me, personally, it was a success. I just wanted there to be new life. I didn't want to acknowledge what I had experienced. And in some ways I felt guilty. For the most part, I was on a pretty safe base. I mean, we went out and did clean-up of mid-air collisions and things that had been shot down or escorted body bags out. I had a sense I hadn't done enough, but I also had a sense of meaninglessness. . . . I started to get a sense of "What does it all mean? Why does it all matter?"

"Bad things happen to good people." I heard that all the time in church but I didn't actually believe it. I believed bad things happen to people who don't pray enough—people God wants to make an example out of. But it wouldn't happen to me because me and God are cool. But now it felt like the God I knew from growing up wasn't even around.

It's no wonder Joe experienced disillusionment after coming back from a traumatic deployment only to be met with more destruction and disorder in the natural world. He left an ordered life to go to a war zone, only to return to a different kind of chaos. Those impractical (and ultimately very costly) blueberry plants were an effort to claw his way back to a God he understood. If his old ideas about God no longer worked, he could start at the most basic beginning point—creation—and work from there.

When we approach God with expectations accumulated through personal bias and cultural lenses, we are penning the Almighty into a limited understanding of who God is and how God operates. What Joe describes is a dismantling of the prosperity gospel teachings that managed to creep their way into modern evangelicalism, as we discussed in chapter 4, despite a collective rejection of anything by that name. Even though the message—"God wants you to be prosperous, so the more faithful you are the more you will be blessed with material success"—may not be as blatant from the average pulpit as it is from slick televangelists, the theology in many of our churches is rooted in the same basic premise: if you do certain things, life will go right by you; if things are not going your way, it must mean that you have not been faithful enough, prayerful enough, or good enough to merit God's favor. In

> *If his old ideas about God no longer worked, he could start at the most basic beginning point—creation—and work from there.*

short, the reasoning goes, bad things happen to bad people because they deserve it; good things happen to good people because God owes us. When God feels absent, it is because we were somehow not *enough* to hold God's attention or secure blessings, and the mere act of acknowledging that God feels absent only puts the believer in a deeper state of sin. It's a vicious cycle that can allegedly only be broken by pouring more time, energy, and resources into church. In short, it's the vile idea of investing in God.

The Bible is full of promises that shape our worldview. We build our theologies on the anticipation of those promise passages playing out in a certain way, pinning our beliefs on what we hope is true and becoming deeply disillusioned when things fail to match our plan. We create God in our own image and feel betrayed when God acts contrary to the ground rules we believe ought to be followed. This is especially difficult when we find him falling short of our expectations of what divine intervention looks like. God's silence feels like absence. But perhaps God is making us uncomfortable to force us to move to a better place.

It's the vile idea of investing in God.

A number of coastal communities ban external lights during sea turtle hatching season. Porch lamps can lure the baby turtles inland, away from the safety of the water, if they mistake the glow of the lightbulbs for the reflection of stars on the ocean. Simply by darkening the lights for a season, homeowners can help the hatchlings make their way to the sea. Put another way, if your cup is empty, you go to your water bottle. If your water bottle is empty, you go to the faucet. If the faucet fails to work, you check the pipes or the well. The emptiness is not a punishment—it's simply the thing that eventually leads us back to the source. Maybe God's apparent absence or silence is really a mercy to draw us away from a place that isn't right for us—a place where we don't belong—into a space that is better.

This was true for Joe, who found that his experience led him to an entirely new relationship with God than the one he grew up with.

I do still have a deep faith in something that's mysterious and bigger than us, but it's also not American and it's not capitalism and it's not transactional. What happens when we try to control our fate too much or assert too much meaning? I'm really proud of where I'm from and my heritage, but to tame the wild and tame the west and control everything is an American idea, I don't think it's a Christian idea. And I think sometimes I confused my national heritage, and my sense of being able to assert control through personal responsibility. It's something that probably perverted the faith that I held.

So when things don't go the way you think they should, just try harder or believe more or pray more or give more or volunteer more because the big Sky God rewards those who do. That's a horrible way to view God because what does that mean for the person who gets cancer or the person who has a sick spouse or mental health challenges? That's not your fault. That doesn't mean you didn't do enough or try hard enough. I just think that a lot of the ways I looked at sex, money, accomplishment, were based on something I don't think is what the Carpenter taught, and I really had to go figure that out.

The God that I had grown up with was gone now. At that point, my understanding of God was probably one of the most immature things about me. I probably had a plastic Jesus, buddy-God, good-luck-charm God—or I spoke enough of the vocabulary but really I was just parroting. . . . Somehow I thought certain things were birthrights instead of blessings. There is a big difference between being abandoned by God and being betrayed by your own immature understanding of God.

o o o

In John 11, we read about the death of Lazarus. Mary and Martha send a message to Jesus informing him that their brother is severely ill, yet Jesus waits two full days before departing to see the family. By the time he arrives, Lazarus had already been in the tomb for four days. Both sisters, independent of one another, greet Jesus with the same words: "Lord, if you had been here, my brother would not have died" (John 11:21, 32). Interestingly, Jesus responds to each sister's charge of neglect differently. He engages type-A, ministry-focused Martha in a conversation that ultimately leads her to make the pronouncement: "Yes, Lord, I believe that you are the Messiah, the Son of God, the one coming into the world" (11:27). With Mary, on the other hand, the more emotion-driven of the sisters, the exchange is different. When she hears that Jesus is approaching the village, she leaves the house where she has been surrounded by mourners and hurries to meet Jesus in the road and kneel at his feet before making her accusation (11:31-32). For Martha, Jesus used his absence to lead her to a new intellectual realization; for Mary, he drew her away from a house filled with weeping people to the road, where she could respond to him on her own terms, unencumbered by the emotional displays around her. Then she led him to the tomb, where the miracle took place. In neither case was the woman reprimanded for challenging Jesus for his absence, but in both cases she was led to a different space that culminated with a new and deeper understanding of who Jesus was.

When the Lord does not seem present in the way we believe God ought to be, it does not mean that we have been rejected or that our faith was not sufficient for God's attention. It means either that God is stepping back slightly—temporarily—to test us, or that God has someplace else, somewhere farther along, toward which we are being called. Detecting this change in God's presence and finding the courage to point it out does not mean that you are lacking in faith, knowledge, or wisdom, and it certainly does not indicate a moral failing on your part. If anything, silence from God may be an indication that you are mature enough to

If anything, silence from God may be an indication that you are mature enough to let go of immature expectations and encounter another, deeper, facet of the Creator of the universe.

let go of immature expectations and encounter another, deeper, facet of the Creator of the universe.

This is, of course, small comfort in the midst of pain, trauma, or the immediacy of loss, but it does mean that God's eye is still upon us despite all tangible evidence to the contrary. After all, what good is a test if the subject is not observed, and what good is a guide who does not check to see if anyone is following? Unfortunately, there is no way to know how long the test may last or just how far our journey to this new place of understanding will take us. Sometimes circumstances are simply terrible and there is simply no good answer why. But that does not mean that God has abandoned us in any permanent way; it is only our old image of God that has proven insufficient. God is not letting go of us; we are being encouraged to let go of our old, outdated, or inaccurate ideas of who he is.

8

ABSENCE:
THE GOD WHO NEVER WAS

Matthew 11:2–15

"I just don't understand it," my friend remarked in our Sunday night small-group meeting. "I've been studying with a coworker for the past three months, but he still refuses to believe in God. He asks all the right questions, and he is such a fundamentally good and loving person; I just don't understand how anyone can be so stubborn."

I shook my head sadly and added that unbelieving coworker to our prayer list of other souls who were not yet saved or had fallen away from their faith, but that specific conversation stayed with me for reasons I couldn't quite name at the time. *Such a shame,* I thought. *Of course, some people struggle with things like assurance, but why would so many people willingly keep themselves from God?*

It wasn't until several years later that it finally occurred to me why that comment had affected me so much. My friend took it for granted that anyone without faith was making a deliberate decision to be in rebellion. All the churches I knew growing up took that same stance: people from other faiths were simply misguided and needed to be rerouted to Jesus, but atheists were a different story—they deliberately and purposely refused to believe what the rest of us knew to be true. And for what? An excuse to engage in sinful behavior without guilt? To appear intellectually superior? A misguided act of rebellion against parents or society? Most likely, yes—all of those, we concluded.

It's embarrassing to admit now, but it wasn't until I was in my midthirties that it even occurred to me that maybe belief is not a choice—that maybe the basic acceptance that there is a divine Presence in our world is not inherent to all people, that maybe Blaise Pascal's proverbial God-shaped hole in the human heart was a bit optimistic, that maybe some genuinely good people have wrestled with the question of God and still come up empty-handed. It took me another decade before it finally occurred to me that maybe not everyone wrestles, either. Maybe doubt isn't a struggle for them—it's not something that plagues them or weighs heavily on their soul; in fact, for some people doubt is something they are quite content with or don't even think about at all.

Yet in our churches, doubt is often feared, frowned upon, viewed as a character flaw, or, at best, waved away as a passing act of rebellion. But what if faith isn't the default setting for all of humanity? What if some people feel their faith slip away even as they fight desperately, but ultimately futilely, to hang onto it? What if some people have *never* felt certainty? What if all who ask, seek, and knock don't actually end up finding God after all?

○ ○ ○

As John the Baptist awaits his execution, he learns of the growing reputation of his cousin Jesus and sends two disciples to ask him, "Are you the one who is to come, or are we to wait for another?" (Matt. 11:3). John's inquiry unapologetically exhibits doubt that Jesus is who he claims to be—which is understandable, given the circumstances; after all, if anyone could reasonably expect a spare miracle to be tossed their way, surely it was Jesus's own cousin. Yet John finds himself languishing in prison, caught in the crosshairs of a political dispute between two sociopathic power players. No wonder he began to question Jesus. John's circumstances didn't look anything like what he must have expected.

Doubt can strike anyone, and it is not a sign of weakness, despite what we may have been taught. John ranks among the bravest and boldest souls in the New Testament, and even he questioned—not because he was somehow weak or rebellious, but because he wanted to make sure that he was being intellectually honest with his life and faith. Doubt requires bravery, because it means admitting that there is a chance that you could be wrong. What if all the systems upon which you built your life were in error? What if it turns out that God wasn't actually there at all?

There seem to be several different paths to doubt: those who gradually find themselves raising more and more questions as time passes, those who abandon all belief in an instant, and those for whom doubt has always been present, an unbidden companion in their spiritual life. For some, the doubts simply become a part of their faith, a permanent element that is as much a part of their relationship with God as trust, prayer, and praise. For others, however, the doubts may reroute their entire path, prompting the deconstruction of an edifice that is never rebuilt on the old foundation.

Ava, one of my college roommates, has wrestled with her belief for most of her life. Raised in a devout family, she wasn't sure what to make of her doubts as a child; now, as a practicing veterinarian, she views her profession as part of the source of her questioning. "I have a scientific brain; that's just the way I see and understand the world," she explains. "I need proof. When I consider that the brain can be chemically altered, it opens a whole can of worms because then I wonder if belief can be chemically altered. Sometimes I'm not sure if I believe in God or if medicine simply made me believe in God."

Ava's conversation with doubt persisted throughout much of

her adolescence and has continued for her entire adult life. For a long time, she was afraid of her doubts and tried to quiet them by acting contrary to what they were telling her: "My fear always overcame my shame. I don't know how many times I went down for the altar call or witnessed to someone, no matter how awkwardly or uncomfortably I did it, because that's what you're supposed to do. So that proved I believed, right?"

Eventually Ava gave up on her efforts to (in her words) "get in good with Jesus." Instead, she now pours her energy into treating her animal patients and working with their families, putting whatever love and care she can into alleviating pain and fighting to preserve life. In this way she shifts her energy from feeding her unresolvable questions to meeting needs. "That's how I can see that I have grown, I have produced fruit," she says. Ava has chosen to accept that while she cannot force herself to believe, she can at least cling to her *desire* to believe and hope that it is "enough" for God in its own way.

> The doubt is there, I think I've just learned to live with it. In my 3 a.m. thoughts, sometimes those doubts become louder. I try to drown them out, like saying the Lord's Prayer, but that usually just feels like throwing words at the wall. I keep trying, hoping that the doubt will someday go away, and I think it's lessened over time, but it's been thirty years so I really think it has more to do with age, fatigue—I just don't have as much energy to throw at it anymore. I just have to live with it as it is. I don't like the 3 a.m. thoughts, because that's when my brain gets caught up in all the what-ifs. I picture myself on my deathbed and—what if there's nothing? Nobody can fix that. Nobody can give me an answer to that. I've talked to enough preachers and done counseling and read enough books and read my Bible all in the hopes that it would fix that, but it hasn't. I'm not sure I'm ever going to get over this. I will probably be ninety-five, on my deathbed, crossing my fingers.

Ava's doubt has challenged her to accept more ambiguity, to be more comfortable with the mystery, and to humbly admit that the hymn "Blessed Assurance" will never really ring true for her, though she continues to sing it every Sunday. Doubt is the very thing that has made her faith stronger because she is determined to persist in spite of it. But for others, doubt can lead to a very different outcome.

In the 1946 short story "Antaeus," by Borden Deal, a young boy who moved from the rural South to Chicago during the Depression finds joy in a small patch of grass he plants on top of his apartment building. His happiness is fleeting, however, when the soil and water cause the ceiling below to sag, which lands him in trouble. As he flings clump after clump off the roof, the narrator notes, "The task of destruction is infinitely easier than that of creation."

It's a lovely line, and true—mostly. It takes a long time to grow a garden, to build up trust, to establish a career, to raise a child, and all that work can be snuffed out in an instant. But sometimes the act of destruction is a slow, gradual process that chips away at certainties and promises until the whole carefully constructed creation comes tumbling down. That's the way faith deconstruction often happens, too. You have a set of beliefs around which you have organized your life, and then, one by one, they all begin to crumble, fade, or fracture. Doubt is the opposite of a God who, we are told, spoke universes into existence and brought forth the world from a vast and empty void. Doubt is *nothing* from *something*.

Many of us were raised on the definition of faith offered in the book of Hebrews: "Now faith is the assurance of things hoped for, the conviction of things not seen" (Heb. 11:1). But we still need a reason for the assurance; faith doesn't come from nothing. There has to be some kind of basis for this belief, some "first cause" that prompted us to invest our confidence in this particular thing in the first place. What happens if that hope disappoints, dissipates, or disappears?

Harrison was a devout, three-times-a-week churchgoer who had been heavily invested in the life of his local congregation until he began to wrestle with belief about a decade ago: "I just started realizing that you could be a moral person even if you believe that after you die, you go back to dust, the lights go out, and that's it. I was afraid of that for a long time, but people showed me by example that I could create something meaningful here and now." He slowly began examining more aspects of his faith and came to realize that the most important parts of it—love, justice, lifting up the oppressed—were not held exclusively by Christianity (or any faith, for that matter). If those truths could exist independent of God, Harrison reasoned, then why did he need to maintain his affiliation with a religious movement that had come to stand for so many things he *didn't* believe in?

"I like to think that my deconversion occurred for philosophical rather than social reasons," Harrison explains.

Sometimes, when I mention to Christians that I'm no longer a believer, they'll ask, "Who hurt you?" In their view, if you didn't leave the church because you wanted to live a wild, sinful life, then you must have left because someone in the church hurt you; and they want to try to identify and fix that hurt so that you can be reintegrated again. But I really don't believe that I was hurt directly by anyone in the church. I've known plenty of people who have been hurt directly by the church, but I don't see myself as one of them. Rather, I think I left because I couldn't contain the cognitive dissonance anymore, because I could no longer blindly accept the moral codes that made no sense or the contradictions that refused to be resolved, because I wanted a worldview that was consistent with itself and with science and with my own lived experience.

He was open with his wife, but it took him nearly three years to admit to his parents that he was agnostic. "I didn't want them to feel they had failed as parents," he said. His mother eventually came to accept his position fairly well, "even if she doesn't agree." He continued, "My dad, on the other hand, has been in something akin to denial, I think. He's mentioned several times that he thinks I'm going through a 'dark night of the soul' or a 'period of doubt,' as though I'll eventually come out on the other side of this phase as a good Christian again. I'm not precluding the possibility that I might someday return to the faith, but I feel that I'm in a very good place right now, a healthy place, and I feel neither need nor desire to return."

Harrison's story is likely familiar to anyone going through a faith deconstruction. As he dismantled old belief systems, he found they no longer aligned with his values; and given the choice between dogma and values, he chose what he felt was the more moral path. While some people may emerge from a faith deconstruction with anger or bitterness toward their former denomination, Christianity, or the concept of God they have left behind, many actually feel freer, healthier, and more hopeful as a result of where their doubt eventually led them. This is true for Harrison; he isn't anti-God, nor does he find the Jesus of the Bible offensive. He takes a pragmatic view, rooted in the outcome rather than the process: "I'd say I'm a hoper, but not a believer. If there is a God and Jesus is his son, I'm happy with that. That means that there will be justice and things will be set right, and that does appeal to me. But most Christians are so uncomfortable with doubt that they would rather say, 'God has it all figured out' and leave it at that."

Many Christians *are* uncomfortable with doubt, and many more are likely to dismiss it with the wave of a hand or else double-down in the hopes of eradicating it before it can take root; such a response, however, can easily backfire. Diane, a dedicated homeschool mother and public library advocate, was raised in a religious tradition that stigmatized doubt so strongly that honest questioning felt like a slippery slope toward a complete rejection of anything religious; as a result, she found herself questioning her faith even more as she fought to deny what she was feeling. Churches and "religious folks" tend to panic at the first sign that someone's faith isn't rock solid, so they often respond by piling on every Scripture, prayer, and argument they can think of rather than realizing that spiritual growth will always involve shifting, and sometimes shedding, beliefs. "Every moment of doubt does not have to be a catastrophe of faith. That's not sustainable. It's wrong to force a crisis of faith on someone who isn't having one," she insists.

As Diane began her own process of faith deconstruction and reconstruction, she initially responded in a similar way to how she had always seen the matter handled in churches: "When I first started questioning, I felt like I had to have answers—and the rights answers—or everything would fall apart. *Everything* felt like it had eternal significance. I wasn't used to doubt, so it just felt so large and threatening." With time, however, she found that the matters of faith with which she was struggling didn't actually have to be a struggle at all; they could simply be questions for which she did not have answers. They did not need to threaten her entire existence. As she let go of the *fear* of doubt, the doubts themselves suddenly seemed to lose their power and became less threatening: "Doubt didn't feel like doubt with a capital D anymore. It was less that I was questioning God himself and more than I was pulling apart the tapestry of my faith to see what held and what was a loose thread. . . . When I no longer felt attached to any one system of theology, the fear of being wrong left and I could just ask. Any God I was invested in would have grace, and grace for this very human feeling of doubt."

> *Every moment of doubt does not have to be a catastrophe of faith.*

o o o

Ava, Harrison, and Diane all found different ways to respond to their doubt. Ava managed to reconcile her struggles with the practice of her faith; Harrison released the struggle altogether; Diane learned to embrace the mystery. However, they all realized that they had to find a way to be honest about doubt rather than trying to explain it away or trying to shame it out of themselves. None of them ever "cured" their doubt; they just converted it into a form that they could live with and carried on in the most life-affirming and love-filled way they could.

In 1 Corinthians 13, the famous "love chapter," the apostle Paul punctuates his words on love with this simple statement: "And now faith, hope, and love abide, these three; and the greatest of these is love" (13:13). The word translated as "faith" (*pistis*) means to believe or to be persuaded that something is true; in fact, it is the primary word in the New Testament for both "faith" and "belief." The word "hope" (*elpis*), however, means to anticipate. In periods of doubt, perhaps *elpis* is the emotion to which we should cling—not the feelings that may or may not ring true, but the anticipation that there is something more than what we can perceive or feel. If we are struggling to have faith in God, maybe we can have faith in *hope* that there is a God, or at least that the ideal that God represents is still the supreme good in the world.

The apostle Paul, widely regarded as the greatest Christian theologian and apologist of all time, states explicitly in God-breathed Scripture that the way we treat people is larger and more significant than what we believe.

But more than traditional faith or even tempered hope, Paul notes that "the greatest of these is love." The word here for "love" (*agapē*) is the Greek word that carries the idea of benevolence, or good will between people—not romantic or brotherly love, but a concern for the wellness of others born out of religious conviction. The apostle Paul, widely regarded as the greatest Christian theologian and apologist of all time, states explicitly in God-breathed Scripture that the way we treat people is larger and more significant than what we believe.

We see this idea repeated again in Galatians 5, where Paul writes about the freedom from legalism that Christ represents. It is not the trappings of faith that carry any meaning; "the only thing that counts is faith working through love" (5:6). Other translations render the word translated here as "working" slightly differently. The basis for the English word "energy," *energeō*, literally means to accomplish or to show activity in a visible or measurable way. The NIV says, "The only thing that counts is faith expressing itself through love," while the NIRV translates it as "faith that shows itself through love." In other words, faith represented through all the traditional outward religious expressions of holiness is not what God wants from us at the end of the day; the only thing that *actually* pleases God is faith/persuasion being carried out through acts of love—not love making itself apparent through faith.

The modern evangelical church has placed so much emphasis on faith versus works that we can easily think of them as a binary. We prioritize Ephesians 2:8–9, "For by grace you have been saved through faith, and this is not your own doing; it is the gift of God—not the result of works, so that no one may boast," in order to make it clear that salvation is not earned. But as a result, we don't always fully consider the implications of such reasoning. Consider the verse again; what is actually given primacy, faith or grace? For those who would demand strict adherence to the text, let us do a close reading: grace is the ultimate driver, faith is just the instrument, not the end goal. The true power is grace, which means kindness or blessings. God's loving mercy toward us is the greater force at work. When we reduce faith to a simple choice we make or don't make, we are turning it into a work—something you do or don't do, or an action to be carried out. The words of Ephesians 2 are not saying that belief is the only thing that brings

God's favor upon us, but that merely going about our daily tasks is nothing to brag about as being pleasing to God. But faith by itself, *sola fide* as it is called in the traditional language of the church, is not the be-all-and-end-all of the Christian faith. As Paul writes in 1 Corinthians 13:2: "And if I have prophetic powers, and understand all mysteries and all knowledge, and if I have all faith, so as to remove mountains, but do not have love, I am nothing." It's the same general idea as James 1:27: "Religion that is pure and undefiled before God, the Father, is this: to care for orphans and widows in their distress, and to keep oneself unstained by the world." The word "religion" translates literally as "worship as expressed in ritual acts." Faith is an engagement with God and God's commands, a dynamic process that will necessarily change and shift as our understanding does. Despite what many of us have heard in churches, faith is not merely a state of belief; it is far more nuanced and complex than something you have or don't have, you embrace or shun, you choose or reject. By itself, "faith" is nothing more than checking a box; it only takes on significance when it is expressed through the way we interact with our world.

> By itself, "faith" is nothing more than checking a box; it only takes on significance when it is expressed through the way we interact with our world.

Maybe, at the end of the day, that's what it comes down to: shades of faith. If we can't hold faith, perhaps we can at least muster hope; if we feel hopeless, we can at least—and at most—love. The way we treat people, the way we offer help rather than judgment, the way we advocate for the voiceless or the silenced, the way we affirm humanity over politics or dogmas, the way we use whatever power we have to give power to other people, too—this is ultimately what matters most.

When we doubt God or question whether God really is whatever we were taught to believe God is, we react honestly rather than hiding or denying our uncertainties. This is exactly what we see modeled in Matthew 11, when John sends his message from prison to Jesus. He didn't beat himself up or try to hide his questioning; he went straight to the source and asked plainly. He wasn't ashamed of entertaining the possibility that his faith had been misplaced; he cared enough to wonder if he needed to shift his beliefs. This is an example for all of us: we ask, we wait, we hope, and we do the best we can to remain a force for good within our circumstances.

9

ARBITRARINESS:
THE GOD OF SHIFTING GOALPOSTS

Genesis 22:1; 23:3

*G*od cares more about your holiness than your happiness.
I groaned and shut my laptop to block out the fourth iteration of that expression I'd seen shared on social media in a week. Sometimes the sentiment appeared in looped script, slanting across a field of hazy wildflowers at sunset, the light artfully overexposed to make everything a little dreamlike. At other times it was spelled out in white plastic letters pushed into a miniature black marquee propped up against a subway tile backsplash. Once it was hastily stenciled in steel gray, the words barking through the screen like a drill instructor dressing down a soft recruit. The correlation between the background and the phrase was never completely clear, but the meaning was unmistakable: your personal concerns are secondary to God's will, and any dissatisfaction you feel in your life is rooted entirely in selfish desires. It's the perfect Christian social media zinger: it feels subversive, bold, countercultural. It has *alliteration*.

And whether it's set in loopy script or just on a repeating loop in our heads, the meaning is unmistakable. The words challenge us to examine ourselves critically—to question our motives and audit our desires. They remind us that when our will fails to align with God's will, God's will has to win out. These words seem equal parts sage advice and tough love, like when your grandma shares her biscuit recipe but then guilt-trips you for not calling enough.

What we hear is the message that "God doesn't care if you are happy as long as you are sticking to the Bible. You'll never be happy if you don't pursue absolute righteousness." And when we hear that, we may find ourselves suppressing our intuition or ignoring the voice warning us that maybe our current conditions—like our job, relationship, or lifestyle—may not be God's best for us. Because we know what we've been taught all our lives in Sunday school about contentedness: good Christians persevere through any circumstance; it's not *this* life that matters, anyway. We're supposed to be concerned with our "treasures in heaven," right? And the greater our suffering here, the greater our reward there. Holiness supersedes happiness every time. Holiness, the ultimate trump card.

Except that it's not.

In Leviticus 18:5 we read, "You shall keep my statutes and my ordinances; by doing so one shall live." It is this verse that forms the basis of the fundamental Jewish principle of *pikuach nefesh*, translated literally as "saving a life." Aside from worshiping other gods or engaging in taboo sexual activity, any moral law comes secondary to the preservation of human life—and when in doubt, a faithful person is supposed to err on the side of caution, with life coming before the law. In other words, an observant Jew is permitted to call 9-1-1 on the Sabbath even though dialing a phone is normally forbidden on that day under Jewish law.

> *The purpose of the law is to give life, not to allow death to prevail over a technicality.*

Or if a person is starving and only unkosher food is available, they can eat it without becoming unclean. The purpose of the law is to give life, not to allow death to prevail over a technicality.

In fact, not only are these violations of law permitted, they are considered a greater act of holiness than adhering to the commandments. A person who places higher priority on saving a life is considered more pleasing to God than one who avoids doing so in an effort to preserve their own religious purity. In fact, the principle of *saving a life* is so sacred that when two people must choose which one violates a religious law to save a life, the more righteous or religiously strict individual is supposed to have the *honor* of doing so.

This extends to the personal level, too. If someone has a condition like diabetes or is on medication that requires food or drink, life takes precedence over religious dictates, even during a fast or on a high holy day. The principle behind this reasoning is common sense: God cares more about the health of God's people than about the minutiae of the law. If food is required for preserving health, then a reasonable amount is permitted, no questions asked.

The idea behind *saving a life* has been part of the Judeo-Christian tradition for at least three thousand years. It is at work in 1 Samuel 21, when David and his men—starving as they evade capture by King Saul—eat the showbread consecrated for the priests. A millennium later, when Jesus and his disciples are challenged for rubbing wheat between their hands on the Sabbath, Jesus points to that same story and cites the prophet Hosea, saying, "I desire mercy and not sacrifice" (Matt. 12:1-8).

And this is far from the only instance where we see Jesus evoke this same idea. In Matthew 12 and Mark 3, he enters the synagogue and heals a man with a withered hand. When confronted by the Pharisees, "Jesus asked them, 'Which is lawful on the Sabbath: to do good or to do evil, to save life or to kill?'" The pattern repeats again in Luke 13, when Jesus breaks the Sabbath by healing the woman whose back has been bent for eighteen years. And yet again when he challenges the Pharisees, asking: "If one of you has a child or an ox that has fallen into a well, will you not immediately pull it out on a sabbath day?" (Luke 14:5). And again when Jesus breaks Jewish religious laws by touching a dead body to raise a little girl (Matt. 9:25; Mark 5:41; Luke 8:54), and when Jesus has physical contact with a leper to heal him (Matt. 8:3; Mark 1:41; Luke 5:13).

Perhaps most strikingly, Jesus evokes the principle of *saving a life* in John 8, with the woman caught in adultery. When the teachers of the law demand that she be executed, Jesus famously challenges the crowd, "Let he who is without sin cast the first stone." And when there are no takers to his offer and the accusers have dispersed, Jesus turns to the woman and tells her, "Neither do I condemn you. Now go and sin no more." He protects the woman's life first, *then* encourages her to pursue holiness. Life takes priority; holiness follows.

Does God care about our holiness? Yes, of course, but it also seems safe to say that God cares *more* about our healthiness. Jesus illustrates over and over that achieving and maintaining mental and physical safety should take priority over any kind of religious conviction. *Saving a life* is not a loophole—it's an injunction. It is the ultimate challenge to us to make life-affirming decisions. We honor God more by choosing life than we do by a legalistic adherence to the law.

It's churches that open an hour late on icy mornings to allow the roads to thaw for the safety of their members or move services online to help stem the pace of a deadly virus. But if this principle of *saving a life* runs throughout the Bible, rests at the heart of Jesus's teaching, and even is present in our own operational thinking of the church, why have so many of us neglected this principle in modern theology?

Maybe it's because of the inherent conflict between "being crucified with Christ" and having life "abundantly." There is suffering implicit in Jesus's command to "take up your cross and follow me," and we embrace that. Suffering endured becomes its own form of sanctification; *struggle* becomes central to the pursuit of holiness. We point to verses like 1 Peter 4:13: "Rejoice insofar as you are sharing Christ's sufferings, so that you may also be glad and shout for joy when his glory is revealed." This passage of Scripture is referring specifically to physical persecution and martyrdom on behalf of the gospel, yet many of us have somehow embraced it to apply to *any* suffering in our lives.

We have separated happiness and holiness, as if true holiness can only be achieved through anguish or a *rejection* of happiness. But here again we draw a sharp distinction between "happiness," which is only temporary and earthly, and "joy," which is transcendent and focused heavenward. *Happiness* is viewed as something ephemeral—pleasure derived from an enjoyable event or object. *Joy*, on the other hand, is that deep-seated feeling of contentment, peace, and delight in the eternal promises of God. Happiness is cotton candy; joy is Thanksgiving dinner and three types of pie for dessert.

The only problem is that this is an artificial distinction. Of the thirteen words translated as "joy" or "rejoice" in the Bible, not one of them has a meaning rooted in duration, and there is no separate word in Hebrew or Greek for "happiness." The differences between the words exist only in the ways in which the joy or rejoicing is expressed, not in how long the feelings last or in the object of the emotion. By creating a discrepancy between happiness and joy that the biblical writers themselves never draw, we modern believers enable ourselves to explain away the apparent paradox that both suffering and joy exist at the heart of the Christian experience. If we consign the notion of happiness to the realm of the fleeting, trivial, or shallow, we can dismiss it as a worldly pursuit that is not nearly as important as our pain. Pain equals holiness after all, right?

When we measure our spiritual success in terms of how much we have suffered for the sake of the gospel, how unpleasant our daily battle against sin is, or how exhaustive our devotion, we are stripping ourselves of the sacred gift of delight.

Happiness in itself is not bad, we insist, but it cannot be equated with holiness; holiness must stand apart as something entirely separate from present pleasure. We often tell ourselves that the only type of joy allowed in the pursuit of sanctification is the joy of the life to come—none of this "feeling good today" nonsense. But what an absurd, puritanical philosophy it is to willingly reject joy.

Cultivating deep-seated joy to carry us through the painful times of life is absolutely a praiseworthy pursuit, but in no way does it mean that God is uninterested in our day-to-day happiness. When we measure our spiritual success in terms of how much we have suffered for the sake of the gospel, how unpleasant our daily battle against sin is, or how exhaustive our devotion, we are stripping ourselves of the sacred gift of delight.

Releasing superficial pleasures in favor of more substantial pursuits is absolutely a calling of the Christian life, but *it does not mean* God doesn't care about our happiness in the long *or* short term. In our well-intentioned commitment of "death to self" and submitting entirely to the Lord, we often prioritize incorrectly. By relegating happiness to some second or third tier of blessings, we deny the goodness that God has created in the world. Instead of the false dichotomy of "God cares more about your holiness than your happiness," the equation looks more like an interdependent triumvirate:

> Happiness without holiness is **hedonism**; it becomes pleasure for pleasure's sake alone.
>
> Holiness without healthiness is **fanaticism**; it is unchecked obsession.
>
> Healthiness without happiness is **pointless**; you're preserving life, but for what purpose?

So, what does this mean for people who seek to honor God?

It means that, like David and like Jesus, we should focus on life and health before we worry about strict adherence to the law.

We need to recognize any unhealthy situations, relationships, circumstances, or behaviors that are oppressing us, regardless of their place in our life or their impact on our reputation as a Christian.

"Healthy" is not a destructive relationship.

"Healthy" is not a church that misuses power.

"Healthy" is not an abusive boss or a toxic work environment.

"Healthy" is not self-harm.

It's not a problematic relationship with food or a lifestyle that consists only of binge watching TV or hours and hours of gaming.

It's not a lack of healthy sexual attitudes or boundaries.

It's not a party lifestyle where substances numb the pain.

It's not binge drinking, binge shopping, or any other type of addiction.

It's not unchecked jealousy.

It's not untreated depression, obsessive compulsive disorder, anxiety, or panic attacks because someone said you should be able to "power through with prayer."

If you try to be holy without first asking yourself whether you are healthy, you can easily slip into a faith that is based in anxiety, fear, or shame. Many of us have been taught that the gospel has to be firmly in place before healing can begin—that hurting persons need to accept Christ first and focus on righteousness *before* they can begin to heal the brokenness or pain in their lives. This is the message we often hear at the end of sermons and in personal testimonies: "I was a mess until Jesus found me. And only after I accepted the cross did I have the tools to put myself back together." Yes, this may be true for many people, but it's by no means an absolute. For some, the path toward righteousness is clouded by unhealthy distractions; it is not until such persons are able to clear the obstructions

> *If you try to be holy without first asking yourself whether you are healthy, you can easily slip into a faith that is based in anxiety, fear, or shame.*

to their *health* that they can see the way forward toward more godly living. To insist on holiness as a prerequisite to healing is akin to missionaries who promise to deliver food to starving people *only if they are baptized first*. It is not only misguided; it is immoral.

And what of the individuals who already have the gospel fixed firmly at the forefront of their lives? People whose well-intentioned desire for holiness is the very thing that is keeping them locked in unhealthy patterns? Tameika, a bioengineer, explains her experience with this type of thinking:

> My parents were very controlling people. . . . I couldn't just be on honor roll at school or a good kid at church. I had to be the smartest, most popular, and best behaved. I picked my college based on the school they liked. I even picked my major and career path based on what they insisted was best. If they expressed a negative opinion about something, even if it was something as innocent as the color of a shirt, I changed to whatever their preference was.
>
> I happily accepted all of these pressures because I believed it was my duty to the Lord. By honoring my father and mother, I was honoring my heavenly Father. What I didn't see was that my parents . . . had made me a codependent adult and also miserable in the process.

When I ask Tameika how this unhealthy relationship with her parents affected her spiritual walk, she pauses a moment before answering:

> Have you ever heard the expression "grandchild of God"—someone who inherited their parents' faith instead of having their own relationship with God? That's what I was. I was a grandchild of God. I was always living under the umbrella of someone else's faith and someone else's Christian walk, trying to convince myself it was my own.

What I believed was making me right with God—catering
to all their wishes, I mean—was actually making me really unhealthy because I didn't even have an idea about my own pref-
erences or spiritual gifts anymore. I inherited all their beliefs
and also all their hang-ups. . . . Anything lacking in my life was
because I wasn't right with God yet, supposedly. I didn't even
realize that the relationship was unhealthy because so much
Scripture and preaching and even cultural pressures told me
I owed my elders any deference they demanded, even when I
was an adult.

"When did you finally prioritize health first, whatever that
meant for how you perceived your spiritual walk?" I ask her.

"Honestly? It wasn't until just a couple of years ago." Tameika
rubs her hand across her face, as if wiping away the embarrass-
ment of her response:

That sounds so bad to say out loud, that it took me into my
forties to actually stop depending on my parents' approval for
everything. But I started to recognize how intrusive their opinions still were in my life, even in my personal relationships.
I finally cut the apron strings of guilt but worried the whole
time that the fury of God was somehow going to come crashing down on me for rejecting my parents' control. Instead of
fury, I suddenly felt a sense of comfort and being at home with
my own beliefs and even my doubts, too. It was like I had been
wearing a mask for all those years and I could finally drop the
act and just be myself with God. I didn't agonize over decisions
in the same way because I wasn't trying to factor in the additional opinions of my mom and dad in a decision that was really
just between me and God.

Distancing oneself, as Tameika did, from the source of a damaging relationship is, perhaps, the most effective step we can take

in pursuing health. Whether through counseling, behavioral therapy, sheer willpower, or even a physical change of address or workplace, separation from the destructive behavior is one of the most essential steps in ending it.

Consider the biblical matriarch Sarah for a moment. In Genesis 22, we read about the sacrifice of Isaac. Then, chapter 23 opens this way:

> Sarah lived to be a hundred and twenty-seven years old. She died at Kiriath Arba (that is, Hebron) in the land of Canaan, and Abraham went to mourn for Sarah and to weep over her.
>
> Then Abraham rose from beside his dead wife and spoke to the Hittites. He said, "I am a foreigner and stranger among you. Sell me some property for a burial site here so I can bury my dead." (23:1–4 NIV)

It's easy to overlook a crucial detail in this passage: Sarah was *not* living with Abraham at the time that she died.

After setting out from her homeland, twice being traded by her own husband to powerful men for material gain (Gen. 12; 20), after seeing her husband father a child with another woman, and watching *her* only child be led away to be killed in a ritual sacrifice—Sarah left. She created distance. At some point, she moved roughly thirty-five miles away from Abraham, taking up residence in an area occupied by a foreign tribe. In an action that seems to mirror Abraham's previous separation from Lot over quarrels involving livestock, where the two men take their tents and possessions and go in separate directions (Gen. 13:5–13), Sarah and Abraham appear to have had a parting of ways also. Sometimes, a division is the most life-affirming option, even if it seems counterintuitive.

Mackenzie, a social worker in her late twenties, faced a similar challenge. "I was in an abusive marriage," she said, "but I didn't even realize it at first. All I knew was that I had taken vows in church to stay married to that man, and 'God hates divorce' [Mal. 2:16], so I stuck around."

She pushes up her sleeve to show me her arm, which is covered with small, parallel slashes that have healed into a series of red scars, like hashmarks keeping track of traumas. "I've always had anxiety. I was a cutter in high school," she explains.

> It was just the only way I knew how to deal with pain. So when he hit me or screamed at me or said horrible things, I would just start cutting again to deal with it. I thought staying true to my vows was the most important thing, because that was how I could stay true to God. Somehow, putting up with the pain made me a better Christian or something. Friends tried to tell me [my husband] was going to kill me, but since he hadn't committed adultery, I thought leaving him was just my own selfishness instead of God's plan for me. And since my parents had gotten divorced when I was a kid, I was determined I wouldn't have a failed marriage, too, no matter what.
>
> It wasn't until a coworker finally convinced me to get help for my cutting that I realized that my trying to stick as close as possible to God's Word was actually hurting me. It was like I had to have a fog lifted before I could see clearly that God wanted me to be alive and okay more than he wanted me to be tortured and trapped by a promise I made in a church when I was twenty.

"So would you say God cares more about your healthiness than your holiness?" I ask her.

Mackenzie replies with an emphatic nod: "Absolutely. You can't be holy if you've been reduced to a shell of a person." She pauses, then adds, "Or if you're dead."

Pikuach nefesh empowers us to separate ourselves from the destructive behavior that threatens our well-being. When happiness takes a backseat to holiness without our addressing the issue of health, conditions are prime for self-destruction. It becomes easy to remain in a dangerous situation, choosing pain over and over again, if we believe that the pain somehow consecrates us. A healthy person can recognize the threat; an unhealthy person may believe that healing is impossible to separate from a legalistic adherence to God's will. Health creates the lens through which objective observation is possible. For a person already committed to Christ, the pursuit of health must come *before* the pursuit of deeper holiness.

But how do we determine these boundaries?

In chapter 27 of *Jane Eyre*, Jane finds herself facing exactly this quandary when she is presented with the tempting proposition of running away with Rochester, even though he is already married. As much as she wants to accept his offer to live as his mistress, Jane insists that to do so would violate the moral boundaries she put into place for herself previously—in a time when she was *not* under emotional turmoil. She tells Rochester: "I will keep the law given by God; sanctioned by man. I will hold to the principles received by me when I was sane, and not mad—as I am now. Laws and principles are not for the times when there is no temptation: they are for such moments as this, when body and soul rise in mutiny."

A healthy person can recognize the threat; an unhealthy person may believe that healing is impossible to separate from a legalistic adherence to God's will.

In other words, Jane is saying that religious convictions made in periods of spiritual calm serve as guideposts to steer us through times when our vision is clouded by confusion. This is a brilliantly succinct piece of advice because it recognizes that the mental health of an individual can affect their ability to perceive reality. If you stick to the boundaries you put in place when you were healthy, you can proceed with confidence: "I am feeling really lonely right now but swore I wouldn't text my ex," or "I know today was rough, but I promised myself I would not have more than one glass of wine at dinner," or, in Jane Eyre's case, "I promised myself I would never commit adultery, even if it turns out his wife may be criminally insane and locked up on the third floor of this enormous house and is about to set us all on fire."

We must periodically reexamine our own spiritual boundaries to make sure they are still consistent with our understanding of Scripture. After all, spiritual growth is not an option; we are commanded to mature. And this sometimes means changing our positions.

But sometimes it doesn't. Sometimes the truth we hold to is fixed and immovable—a bedrock belief upon which we build our life and stake our soul. The boundary exists because it is an absolute in our understanding of God. Whatever choices we make in light of that resolution are unconditional.

And then sometimes the boundary itself is not the issue, but the conditions surrounding the conflict are. Do you have the mental and emotional strength to view the situation through healthy eyes? Can you see the broader implications of each option? Are you adequately equipped to evaluate and act based upon a stable and clear-minded position?

When faced with the challenge of making a difficult choice in distressing circumstances, I propose applying the Jane Eyre Decision-Making Flow Chart, found on page 147. We begin with the resolution or boundary that has been challenged, and then ask the essential questions: Was I sane/healthy when I made it? Am I sane/healthy now?

As you become healthier, you will naturally start to become holier.

As you work your way through the chart, a path forward should emerge. Either you have the clarity and perspective to make a healthy, life-affirming decision, or else you need trustworthy, godly guidance to help get you to a place where you can. To enjoy a

Jane Eyre Decision-Making Flow Chart

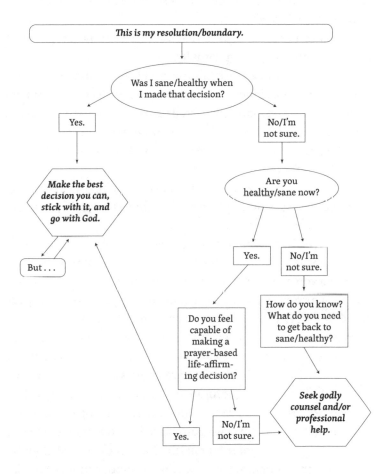

This is my resolution/boundary.

Was I sane/healthy when I made that decision?

Yes.

No/I'm not sure.

Make the best decision you can, stick with it, and go with God.

But . . .

Are you healthy/sane now?

Yes.

No/I'm not sure.

Do you feel capable of making a prayer-based life-affirm-ing decision?

How do you know? What do you need to get back to sane/healthy?

Yes.

No/I'm not sure.

Seek godly counsel and/or professional help.

God-filled existence, health must take the primary position ahead of personal preference or religious mandates: *saving a life*. As you become healthier, you will naturally start to become holier.

When you are out of that demeaning, abusive, or shame-based relationship, you can develop a sense of self-worth in terms of your relationship with God.

When you are in a church that has Christ at its core, instead of power, you can grow spiritually.

When you leave a work environment that causes you to act against your conscience or surrounds you with coworkers who drain life from you, you can instead focus your God-given talents in a way that doesn't compromise your beliefs or best self.

When you are no longer engaging in self-harm, you can honor God with your body.

When you are physically active, eating right, and exercising your body, you are taking care of the vehicle God gave you to get through this life.

When you honor your sexuality in beneficial ways, you are honoring and valuing yourself and the God-given gift of intimacy.

When you no longer feel the need to check out of your life via chemical means, you can assert control over your body and your decisions, moving into a place of wholeness in God.

When you are living within your means, so that you are not in debt or placing your treasure "where rust and thieves can get it," you have resources to relieve suffering, fight for justice, and improve our world.

It is not by accident that Jesus was both a teacher and a healer.

When you have learned how to manage or have gotten medical treatment for your mental health challenges so that they no longer control or define you, you can feel more confident in discerning between the harmful thoughts brought on by your condition and your true beliefs.

When you move first toward being healthy, holiness will follow. But you cannot have genuine holiness without first achieving healthiness. God cares about your holiness *and* your happiness, but God also cares about your healthiness, because it is the pivot upon which everything else turns. It is not by accident that Jesus was both a teacher and a healer. Never let a social media sound-bite convince you that there is anything positive God does not want for you. You cannot be truly holy without first being healthy, and your holiness is a sad legacy if you can find no joy in it.

Healthy, holy, happy. In that order.

ANTAGONISM:
THE GOD OF CHAOS

> Genesis 4:1–17
> Genesis 27:1–45, 31; 33:1–17

"I was really angry for a really long time," Kim said. "Nothing seemed fair; I was searching, but there were no answers."

It was the fall of 2011, and I was catching up with a dear friend about the twists, turns, and unpredictable paths of life over the past few years. After college and following a series of disappointments from God—a severe health crisis and rejection by loved ones and faith groups as he explored his gender identity—Kim eventually fell into a lifestyle marked by substance abuse. After several years, he decided that he wanted to pursue sobriety and eventually landed right back in the small, conservative southern town where we'd both gone to college. The move surprised a number of people, but for Kim, it was an obvious choice: it was the last place he had felt loved and connected to a broader community. He knew there might be objections to his nonbinary gender from some residents, but he also trusted that the love and support of his church would prevail and hoped that his family would choose to reconnect with him one day, too.

Kim found his place in a family of believers who supported and sustained him as he rebuilt his life free from addiction. The last time I saw him, we spoke of the nonprofit work in which he was engaged and his excitement over the direction in which God was guiding his life. He was especially energized about the organization he was working with in a neighboring state designed to help families and churches engage in honest and affirming discussions with and about LGBTQ+ individuals. "I mean, I'd rather be on a beach somewhere," Kim laughed, "but I love these people."

When Kim was killed in a car accident eight months later, hundreds of people showed up to his memorial service, where the eulogists spoke unapologetically of his struggles, triumphs, and identity. No one compared him to the prodigal son; Kim had not come crawling back begging for a place among the servants. He had returned to town with his head held high, proud of his sobriety, proud of the wisdom he'd gained, and happy to claim his place at the table exactly as he was. He made his peace with God, despite the seeming unfairness of some of his challenges that made him sometimes question God's grace.

As I helped pack up his house following the funeral, I was struck by the fact that Kim hadn't decorated with paintings or knickknacks; his main décor was framed photographs—snapshots of himself with the people he loved—set up on nearly every shelf and covering every wall in every room. Despite feeling isolated and rejected in any number of ways, he chose to break free from past hurts and troubles by pursuing meaning and celebrating connection. After years of hurt and anger, Kim created a deeply significant beauty out of the pain he faced.

Kim's story, at its core, is perhaps the oldest story known to humankind. One of the most prolific themes in the literature of the ancient Near East was the tension between order and chaos, especially at the dawn of time. In fact, the very word "chaos" is a transliteration of χάος, the Greek word referring to the shapeless, gaping, or watery void that existed before time began in the creation myths of many ancient cultures. From this space, or "chaos," the gods and goddesses begin separating elements of the earth and ordering their function.

Given this near-universal motif in the cultural context surrounding both ancient Israel and the Greco-Roman world of the first century, it is no surprise that a similar theme is present throughout the sacred texts of ancient Israel and even up through the composition of the New Testament: Jesus's resurrection after a descent into the realm of death is a kind of reordering of a new creation that conquers the chaos of sin and its consequences. Order from chaos is thus one of the most predominant themes throughout Scripture.

In Genesis, however, we see this idea played out the most literally, beginning with the ordered creation in which "the earth was a formless void and darkness covered the face of the deep, while a wind from God swept over the face of the waters. Then God said, 'Let there be light'; and there was light. And God saw that the light was good; and God separated the light from the darkness. God called the light Day, and the darkness he called Night. And there was evening and there was morning, the first day" (1:2-5). And so it goes for five more days, as God methodically pulls design and structure from the primordial soup of the emerging world until, at the end of the sixth day, "God saw everything that he had made, and indeed, it was very good" (1:31). We see the motif played out again and again throughout the text, as the established order (a garden, a ritual sacrifice, a comfortable home, a thriving city, a birthright, a family structure) is somehow disrupted or thrown into chaos (temptation, murder, deception, jealousy), which God then works to restore or rebalance in some different way that launches the story in a new direction. The word "Genesis" means "In the beginning," and it is, indeed, a book of starts and restarts as God continually shapes something better out of disorder. In one of the final lines of the book, Joseph—favored by his father, Jacob; sold by his brothers into slavery; falsely accused and imprisoned; and finally promoted to second in command over all Egypt—sums up this motif when he tells his brothers, "Even though you intended to do harm to me, God intended it for good, in order to preserve a numerous people, as he is doing today" (50:20).

Reading Scripture through the lens of order stemming from chaos, we can find a measure of comfort and reassurance that "We know that all things work together for good for those who love God, who are called according to his purpose" (Rom. 8:28). What do we do, however, when God seems to operate by a set of rules completely unknowable or inscrutable to a human understanding of order? When our world seems governed by the God not of Romans 8 but of Isaiah 55:8, which says,

> For my thoughts are not your thoughts,
>   nor are your ways my ways, says the LORD?

How are we supposed to make order out of chaos when the chaos seems to stem from God's own self, with a set of rules we don't understand, that seem to be enforced inconsistently, or that sometimes even seem intentionally skewed against us?

Perhaps the greatest biblical example of God seeming to operate completely outside of any kind of mutually understood rules of engagement is the story of Cain and Abel. Despite millennia of speculation and theories, from Philo and Josephus to medieval rabbis and Renaissance scholars to Victorian theologians and modern preachers, we still do not know what exactly displeased God so much about Cain's sacrifice. The biblical text offers little in the way of clues; the closest it comes to offering a reason is in 1 John 3:11–12: "For this is the message you have heard from the beginning, that we should love one another. We must not be like Cain who was from the evil one and murdered his brother. And why did he murder him? Because his own deeds were evil and his brother's righteous." But exactly what made Cain's deeds evil and Abel's righteous is left unexplained.

With no definitive answer despite thousands of years of speculation and logical gymnastics to explain why Cain was turned
away, we as readers are left to draw our own conclusions. Ultimately, we tend to give up trying to understand God's reasoning
and move on to Cain's murderous act and subsequent banish-
ment. But in doing so, we may fail to observe two important details: first, that God had mercy on Cain in his exile and gave him
a form of protection (Gen. 4:15), and, secondly, that Cain—the
pariah—does not remain alone forever (4:16–17).

When God confronts Cain about his crime, it is not the all-
encompassing condemnation we are often taught. God is angry
over the bloodshed but does not banish Cain to a violent, isolated
fight for survival. God tells him:

> "When you till the ground, it will no longer yield to you its
> strength; you will be a fugitive and a wanderer on the earth."
> Cain said to the LORD, "My punishment is greater than I can
> bear! Today you have driven me away from the soil, and I shall
> be hidden from your face; I shall be a fugitive and a wanderer
> on the earth, and anyone who meets me may kill me." Then
> the LORD said to him, "Not so! Whoever kills Cain will suffer
> a sevenfold vengeance." And the LORD put a mark on Cain, so
> that no one who came upon him would kill him. Then Cain went
> away from the presence of the LORD, and settled in the land of
> Nod, east of Eden. (4:12–16)

For centuries, the nature of Cain's mark has been debated, parsed,
analyzed, and even distorted by untold generations of scholars.
Likely due to scribes confusing the names "Cain" and "Chaim" (a
transliteration of "Ham," Noah's third son, who was cursed for
disrespect of his father), the ambiguous mark was often referred
to as "the curse of Cain" in theological writing and religious art,
and the two ideas conflated into one. As a result of this tradition,
even modern readers often overlook the fact that the mark was, in
fact, an act of mercy intended to protect him, not a punishment.

Despite the fact that Cain is cast out from his family, God does not leave him empty-handed; in fact, God seems to *increase* allegiance to Cain, by promising "a sevenfold vengeance" on anyone who might kill him.

It is at this point, carrying this extra measure of grace, that Cain steps out into the world. In Genesis 4:17, we get our final glimpse of Cain's life, when the text states that Cain "built a city, and named it Enoch after his son Enoch"—understood tradition-ally as the first city ever established. This passage perfectly encap-sulates the paradox at the heart of Cain's story. He is at once an outcast and wanderer living outside the fold of his family, yet also the father of the original "chosen family," communal living, and, ultimately, civilization. Cain's story culminates not in his rejection or isolation, but in his re-creation of human community.

Through Cain, we see that God does not automatically turn away from us for failing to understand the ways of the Almighty or struggling with the seeming unpredictability of divine prefer-ences and whims. The repercussions may not seem logical or fair, but the separa-tion of an individual from circumstances does not necessarily mean that God has lifted all favor from that person. This is a theme that repeats itself several times in the book of Genesis. For example, within the story of the twins Esau and Jacob, we see parallels to Cain and Abel—a younger brother who seems unfairly favored by God for reasons unstated in the text and an older brother who harbors murderous feelings toward him as a result. In the case of Esau and Jacob, however, it is the younger brother who is cast out.

> *Cain's story culminates not in his rejection or isolation, but in his re-creation of human community.*

If anyone in the story has a right to complain about the sheer chaos of a dysfunctional family structure, it's Esau. His parents each chose a favorite twin, provoking tremendous sibling rivalry between their sons. First he impetuously agrees to sell his birth-right for a bowl of stew, then Jacob, at the urging of their mother, hoodwinks their blind and ailing father by disguising himself as Esau so as to receive the patriarchal blessing. Esau is understandably furious, heartbroken, and desperate for *something* to cling to for his future. In fact, he begs his father three times for a blessing—any blessing—and Isaac finally capitulates, offering his beloved son the following words:

> "See, away from the fatness of the earth shall your
>   home be,
>   and away from the dew of heaven on high.
> By your sword you shall live,
>   and you shall serve your brother;
> but when you break loose,
>   you shall break his yoke from your neck."
>
> (Gen. 27:39–40)

Despite the bleakness of the opening, which casts him far from the bounty of the family's fold, the blessing nevertheless ends on a significant note: Esau will one day escape the power of his brother's influence. And when he does finally succeed, he will forever be free of any control by or burden from Jacob.

That is truly a blessing. Isaac is telling his eldest son that, despite whatever struggle and alienation await him, Esau will eventually be able to let go of the pain. He will throw off the curse Jacob caused him to carry and step out unencumbered by his losses. In short, *Isaac blesses Esau with the power of moving on.* This not a leftover benediction of worthless scraps; this a tremendous act of mercy. This is the greatest wish for the future that Isaac is able to bestow upon his favorite child.

As we see, however, the blessing did not take root immediately. Esau still felt consumed by anger at the injustice of a system that robbed him of his birthright by a contract of questionable legality; he planned to kill Jacob for stealing the original blessing, but Rebekah helped her younger son run away into exile. Twenty years later, however, the text reveals that Isaac's blessing for Esau did in fact come to pass.

When Jacob dares to reenter his family's ancestral land, he sends waves of lavish gifts ahead of him to appease his brother, or perhaps to demonstrate his own might. Upon learning that Esau is riding out to meet him accompanied by four hundred men, however, Jacob is "greatly afraid and distressed" (32:7) and sends up a desperate prayer to God. He begs, "Deliver me, please, from the hand of my brother, from the hand of Esau, for I am afraid of him; he may come and kill us all, the mothers with the children" (32:11). Clearly, Esau is in Jacob's head, so to speak. In fact, it is the night before the dreaded reunion when Jacob has his famous wrestling match with God that ends with Jacob demanding yet another blessing. The following day, as Esau's entourage approaches, Jacob moves to the front of his assembly and "bowed down to the ground seven times, until he came near his brother" (33:3). Jacob is a man beset with anxiety.

This is no gentle setting down of one's pain; it is the act of hurling it off in defiance.

But Esau? He "ran to meet him, and embraced him, and fell on his neck and kissed him, and they wept" (33:4). When the elder brother questions Jacob as to the extravagant gifts, Jacob explains that it was an effort to find favor in his sight. "But Esau said, 'I have enough, my brother; keep what you have for yourself'" (33:9). Esau no longer envied anything that Jacob might possess.

Yes, Esau had let go of the past, but this story is about so much more than the power of forgiveness. Isaac's blessing to Esau was not that the young man would one day soften his heart toward his brother; the image is that of an ox violently overwhelming the weight of the yoke and tearing it from himself by sheer muscle. Isaac did not wish for Esau to gradually capitulate and eventually surrender to his brother's lordship. He told his son that he would one day become "restless" and rebel; he would throw off the burden violently rather than bending to it any longer. This is no gentle setting down of one's pain; it is the act of hurling it off in defiance. Esau liberated himself from the confusing and seemingly anarchic rules of his old life in order to find peace away from the confusing, chaotic restraints that were unfairly placed upon him. Remember: this was Esau's *blessing*.

What we see in Esau is so much more than a man who has let go of past wrongs; we see someone who has finally rejected the brokenness, hurt, and disappointment in his life and has set out to create a world for himself that defies whatever limitations people or circumstances may have placed upon him. He threw off the yoke of an unhealthy relationship and released the bitterness that was, reasonably, his to carry. He rejected the narrative of gaslighting that his difficulties were a result of anything other than parental pettiness and manipulation. He removed the burden that was crushing him rather than sustaining him, and it was this act that allowed him to engage with his former enemy on his own terms.

Each brother comes into the full realization of his blessing on the same day—Jacob, at dawn, when he demands the benediction from God; and Esau, by the ford at Jabbock, in the land of Edom, when he sees his brother face-to-face and knows Jacob no longer holds any power over him. The twin blessings come to fruition in tandem.

How often have we felt this way—surrounded by a world that operates in lawless chaos with a few unknowable rules that may cost us everything or disappointments that almost seem like a personal vendetta? And if we dare to question, we are often shot down, hushed up, or shooed away. We end up feeling robbed of our birthrights of peace and acceptance by those who are supposed to love us and be part of our tribe. Sometimes, painfully, it may seem as if God's favor inexplicably falls on certain people while bypassing us altogether.

Esau's story is a blessing to all rejected peoples: we do not have to live under the control of anyone else. Whether we choose to one day reengage with the person or people who hurt us or choose to cut ties permanently, the point is that it is a *blessing* to break the yoke of someone else's power over us. As the saying goes, the best revenge is a well-lived life. Esau had learned how to live well in letting go of the pain and rejection of his youth. It took time and heartache, but he did eventually succeed in throwing off the burdens of anger and pain from the betrayal of the people around him.

To better understand this kind of defiance-based forgiveness, it will help to examine the concept of the word as it is used in Scripture. The Greek verb *aphiēmi* (literally "to send away") is the primary word used in the New Testament to communicate forgiveness; it appears in verb or noun form more than sixty-five times in this context, and the image is of God casting away our sins from us. Its secondary uses, however, broaden the scope to include the idea of abandonment or separation; for example, Jesus's disciples "abandon" their nets and boats and families to follow him (Matt. 4:20; Mark 1:18–20; Luke 5:11; 18:28–29). The same word is also used to describe someone leaving on a journey or a commission (Mark 12:12), Jesus stepping away from his followers for solitude (Mark 8:13), the way in which thieves leave their victim to die before the Good Samaritan finds him (Luke 10:30), and those who remain behind in the second coming (Luke 17:34–36). Following the final rebuke in Jesus's temptation, this is also the verb used to describe how the devil left Jesus before the angels attended to him (Matt. 4:11). Paul even uses the verb to mean "to divorce" in 1 Corinthians 7:11–13. In other words, it is a word that conveys emphatic removal, omission, separation, and physical distance. God restores order by removing the chaos of sin or brokenness.

In this way, the Greek word "forgive" functions slightly differently than the Old Testament words often translated in association with forgiveness: *nasa* and *kipper*. *Nasa*, meaning "to lift up or carry," is the word Cain uses when he cries out to God that his punishment is "more than [he] can bear." In Genesis 50:17, Joseph's brothers use this verb when they tell him that their father wished for Joseph to forgive his family—that is, to lift the burden of their guilt from them. *Kipper*, on the other hand, means "to cover over, appease, purge." Interestingly, Jacob uses both verbs in Genesis 32:20 as he prepares to meet Esau: "For he thought, 'I may appease [*kipper*] him with the present that goes ahead of me, and afterwards I shall see his face; perhaps he will accept [*nasa*] me.'"

These two Hebrew words both communicate a change in the sin state so that its presence is no longer apparent. In this way, they also function as forgiveness words. By Jesus's time, however, the concept of forgiveness had shifted from a lifting or covering of guilt to denote a physical separation from the offense. In other words, forgiveness, as Jesus taught it, not only encompassed the idea of lessening the load or smoothing it over but also allowed for removal, dismissal, or abandoning—a division between two parties. Reconciliation is certainly encouraged, but reengagement is not required. Forgiveness can sometimes mean leaving something—or someone—behind.

We see this notion of holy separation—of a boundary established peacefully but not necessarily amicably elsewhere in Jacob's story—in Genesis 31. When Jacob takes his wives, children, and vast holdings to leave Laban's employment and return home, Rachel steals the figurines her father Laban kept as household gods. Upon realizing that the statues were missing, Laban pursues the caravan seven days and nearly catches up with it. "But God came to Laban the Aramean in a dream by night, and said to him, 'Take heed that you say not a word to Jacob, either good or bad'" (31:24).

In direct defiance of this charge, Laban approaches Jacob the next day and, after a confrontation, reminds him, "It is in my power to do you harm; but the God of your father spoke to me last night" (31:29). Jacob, in turn, lashes back, countercharging Laban with trickery and false accusations. The chaos that comes from dysfunctional family relationships was certainly a consistent pattern throughout Jacob's life.

The two men eventually agree to establish a pile of rocks stacked into a kind of pillar, called Mizpah (literally, "watch-tower"). After their assembled families help erect the stack, Jacob and Laban send them away and face one another alone over the stones while Laban takes a solemn vow:

> "This heap is a witness between you and me today." Therefore he called it Galeed, and the pillar Mizpah, for he said, "The LORD watch between you and me, when we are absent one from the other. If you ill-treat my daughters, or if you take wives in addition to my daughters, though no one else is with us, remember that God is witness between you and me."
>
> Then Laban said to Jacob, "See this heap and see the pillar, which I have set between you and me. This heap is a witness, and the pillar is a witness, that I will not pass beyond this heap to you, and you will not pass beyond this heap and this pillar to me, for harm. May the God of Abraham and the God of Nahor"—the God of their father—"judge between us." (31:48–53)

The Mizpah, in other words, formed a sacred boundary between two factions in conflict; it signified a God-sealed agreement that neither one would cross the line to harm the other. It restored order by removing the chaos of a wild-goose chase across Mesopotamia by a man bent on revenge, and instead established rules enacted by creating distance.

There may come a time when we have to ask ourselves where we need a Mizpah in our own lives. Where do we recognize an appropriate place to erect a symbolic barrier that does not necessarily negate contact but severely limits it and establishes a nonnegotiable boundary? Is there any area where cutting ties or letting go of a person, situation, or behavior could create order out of the pain?

Both Cain and Esau demonstrate the beauty of moving on from a painful past and choosing to create a new life. In Cain's case, he is credited with establishing the first city, marking a shift from a clannish, hunter-gatherer system to a communal and collective way of life determined less by blood ties and more by what each member contributes to the society. Similarly, Esau's greatest triumph was not only that he shook off the yoke but also what he did afterward. He marched out to meet Jacob with an entourage for support and security, and as a show of force; no matter how fruitful Isaac and Rebekah's sons may have been, with only twenty years in which to work, there is no way that all four hundred of those men were biological kinsmen. Some certainly were sons, sons-in-law, and servants, of course, but others would have been townsmen from the surrounding cities, members of neighboring tribes, and anyone else from the vicinity of Edom with whom Esau may have had an alliance. Somehow, in some way, Esau—like Cain—formed a community. Each character is traditionally presented as the antagonist in his own story—the person who is set up in opposition to the sympathetic character or the hero (in this case, Abel and Jacob); in standing against their brothers, Cain and Esau are also often painted as if they are standing against God. And yet these men end their narratives surrounded by a deeply fulfilling and blessed life they have built for themselves.

Just because we do not understand the apparent chaos of God's workings does not mean that we are without recourse. It does not mean that we are left to fend for ourselves. It does not mean that we are destined for a life of exile or isolation. It means that we are empowered—even blessed—by the act of overcoming the burdens of our past. Even if we have chaos *of our own making* in our lives, like Cain, that does not mean that the consequences are too great to reconcile, and creating community is one of the most powerful ways to do so. It is one of the most significant ways that we can create order out of anarchy and meaning from mayhem.

Remember, both Cain and Esau received their blessings *after* they challenged their circumstances. Emerging from chaos or dysfunction does not have to mean walking away from God—even if God's name is invoked in the thick of it; the first step in restoring order or seeking peace can be turning *toward* God as a way out.

Community provides structure, support, connection, and safety. Feelings of isolation or being misunderstood in the midst of a system one can't navigate successfully can lead to acts of violence. There is a common saying in substance-abuse circles: "The opposite of addiction is not sobriety, it is connection." Human relationships are the most basic and fundamental way of laying the groundwork for creating an ordered path out of chaos. Community is the reason Alcoholics Anonymous has sponsors and numerous organizations provide mentors for at-risk youth. It should not surprise us, then, to see that both Cain and Esau actively cultivated their own communities once they separated from the dysfunction of their former lives.

> *Emerging from chaos or dysfunction does not have to mean walking away from God—even if God's name is invoked in the thick of it.*

It goes without saying that we must be careful to surround ourselves with those who would seek to build us up and offer humble conversation about God rather than to presume to speak as a divine mouthpiece, like Job's well-intentioned but highly misguided friends did, as we saw in chapter 3. Nor should we simply jump from one unhealthy situation to another until we have lost sight of God altogether. Our relationships themselves should not be a further source of chaos but a kind of micro-Genesis—the creation story told in miniature, as a world in disarray is methodically and deliberately set aright in such a way that it, too, "is very good."

When God's ways seem inscrutable, we must seek out one another—people, like us, who were made in the image of God—to help us wade through the gaping, swirling void of confusion and hurt. When God does not seem to govern through order, we must create that order ourselves by looking for a healthy community that helps us draw some meaning out of the mess. When it feels as if we are pitted against the God we have been taught to fear, we must seek God in those who meet us where we are—not with judgment or manipulation—but with honest engagement and respect for the order we seek to make of our own messy, confusing, dysfunctional stories; blame is rooted in chaos rather than the life-giving restoration of building order. Our objective is not necessarily finding answers but shedding the burdens that threaten to isolate us, just as they did Cain, Esau, and my friend Kim. A community cannot erase our history, but it can help us find our way forward when our blessing and birthright seem to have gone awry. It is through human connection that God calls us to draw on our divinely inspired mercy and love to share, connect, invite, include, affirm, and embrace.

A community cannot erase our history, but it can help us find our way forward when our blessing and birthright seem to have gone awry.

11

ACCOUNTABILITY:
THE GOD WHO EXPECTS US TO ACT

Ruth 1
Lamentations 3

In July of 2005, while I was working as a research assistant on a book about the desegregation of a prominent college athletic program, my job was to find people who had been present at certain sporting events and interview them to learn about their experiences. By posting signs in a few long-standing local businesses around the city, I was able to make some connections. But as one elderly gentleman at a barbershop told me, "If you want to discuss race relations in Birmingham during that time, you need to talk to Chris McNair. He runs a catering business here in town—look him up."

So, putting my faith in a phone number I found on Google, I made a cold call the next morning to Mr. McNair's business and asked if he might have time to meet with me at his convenience later that week. "I'm free now," he said. "Why don't you come on by?"

Less than an hour later I was knocking at a screen door that led to a basement lined with several industrial washers and a short hallway opening onto a large commercial kitchen. "I've got

some linens coming out of the dryer right now," Mr. McNair told
me. "If you don't mind, I'll fold while we talk."

He settled his big frame into a metal folding chair in front of
an open dryer and began pulling cloth napkins out one at a time
as he reflected on his work for social justice during the 1960s and
1970s—of the progress that had been made, but also the great distance yet to go. He remarked how proud he was to be a business
owner now, and how his success in 2005 was something that was
hard to imagine in those days. "I'm a photographer, too," he said.
"Want to see some of my work?"

Napkins all folded, he led me down a hallway hung with beautiful photos of scenes around Birmingham—black-and-white
portraits of weary, lined faces and colorful shots of children
playing jump rope on the sidewalk. Eventually, these works gave
way to some older photos from the civil rights era. "This is one I'm
very proud of," he said, stopping in front of a picture of Martin
Luther King Jr.

"You photographed Dr. King?" I exclaimed. "How wonderful!"

"He came to my daughter's funeral," Mr. NcNair answered
quietly.

There was an awkward pause as I searched for words to cover
my gaffe. "I—I'm so sorry."

"My daughter is Denise McNair," he explained. "She was
the youngest of the girls killed in the 1963 church bombing. She
was eleven."

He must have sensed that I was still struggling for words to
apologize for my ignorance. I knew of the tragedy, of course, but I
had failed to make the connection between it and the man standing before me. "We have some of her things on display upstairs,"
he told me gently. "Why don't you stop and take a look at them
on your way out?"

I thanked him for his time and headed up to the main floor,
where there was a small gallery with a large, framed picture of

Denise hanging on the wall. In the middle of the room was a display case that held her child-sized sewing machine with the doll dress she had been making still pinned beneath the presser foot. Next to that were the shoes she had worn to church that day, her Bible, and the Sunday school worksheet she had been carrying up from class to the sanctuary when the bomb detonated. The little shoes, Bible, and paper were all spattered with blood. Those relics spoke not only of a young girl's life but as testimony to a community that had faced unimaginable and intentional evil.

∘ ∘ ∘

Sometimes God simply doesn't seem to act like God, which can be the biggest betrayal there is. In a world with human trafficking, child abuse, elder abuse, bigotry, racism, sexism, ableism, discrimination, and violent crimes, it may seem like no one is in charge—certainly not an all-loving, all-knowing, all-powerful God.

The question of evil (sometimes called "the problem of pain") and the place of God within it has been debated for millennia. The book of Job, composed sometime between the seventh and fourth centuries BCE, explored this theme. So did the Greek philosopher Epicurus, who is credited with authoring the so-called Epicurus Paradox around 300 BCE:

> Is God willing to prevent evil, but not able? Then he is
> not omnipotent.
> Is he able, but not willing? Then he is malevolent.
> Is he both able and willing? Then whence cometh evil?
> Is he neither able nor willing? Then why call him God?[1]

The early Christian apologist Lactantius tackled the question in the late third and early fourth century CE, while polymath David Hume, a product of the Scottish Enlightenment in the mid-eighteenth century, dissected it perhaps most famously for modern theologians, who are still wrestling with it today.

No issue that has been debated for roughly 2,700 years is likely to be resolved in any satisfactory way here, but that does not mean we are any less likely to continue asking the same questions. But as we discussed in the introduction, this is not a book about answers; this is a book about acknowledging the validity of our questions and recognizing the God-given freedom we have to ask them without shame or fear of rejection by our faith community. We are called to defend truth without backing down or giving in to intimidation—to stare down hate and not blink. Just as Jesus did.

Defiance is part of the gospel, too.

In that light, let us examine two biblical figures who endure a measure of suffering beyond anything it seems a reasonable God would allow, and consider how their responses provide a model for standing up to suffering, whether in the natural world or within a society.

Turning first to Naomi, who announces that "the Almighty has dealt bitterly with me" (Ruth 1:20), we find a woman who takes no pains to hide her discontent with God. When a famine strikes

Defiance is part of the gospel, too.

Judea, she and her husband move with their two sons from Bethlehem to Moab (modern-day Jordan). First, Naomi is widowed, then she loses both of her sons. Naomi is, in many ways, the female version of Job; unlike Job, however, Naomi does not sit in the ashes. When she receives word that the famine has lifted, Naomi resolves to return to her homeland after a decade away and encourages her widowed daughters-in-law to stay with their own people in Moab. Rather than demanding that they follow her back to the land of Israel, as she could have done (women fell under the authority of their husbands' family or tribe when they married), Naomi tells them, "Go back each of you to your mother's house. May the LORD deal kindly with you, as you have dealt with the dead and with me" (Ruth 1:8). Twice she urges them to go home. In this small detail, we see our first hint of Naomi's movement against the problem of pain. Although she knows that she will be lonely and likely more vulnerable on her own, she does not impose her own will on her sons' widows; she demonstrates empathy by telling them to return home—empathy for the young women as well as their mothers. Naomi understands a parent's grief at being irrevocably separated from a child, and she tries to spare anyone else that pain. This is her initial act of defiance: she finds the courage to act in a way that will spare other people the same hurt she is experiencing, no matter the cultural norms.

Naomi's defiance continues. While one daughter-in-law returns home, the other, Ruth, insists on staying with her, and so it is with Ruth by her side that Naomi sets out to leave the land of her suffering and return to her old home in Israel to create a new life for herself. Her trials have stripped her of everything but her own sense of agency; it is precisely because she no longer has a husband or sons to serve that she is free to make the decision to leave Moab and return to Israel. She leverages her societal disadvantages into a means to advocate for herself. She even changes her name when she returns home, announcing:

> "Call me no longer Naomi,
>   call me Mara,
>   for the Almighty has dealt bitterly with me." (1:20)

In fact, she points out the extra measure of suffering she has been handed three times in the opening section of the book (1:13, 20, 21). She does not regard her past as something to just "get over"; she acknowledges its very real influence on her present. Naomi further identifies her influential kinsman and devises a plan to win his advocacy on behalf of her family. She is a tenacious, determined force who is always thinking one step ahead of her current circumstances.

Jeremiah has a complaint for God that is similar to Naomi's, but his story is of a man at his breaking point, soul-tired from bowing to God's commands again and again, only to be persecuted, mocked, and humiliated at each turn. He is finally pushed to the edge, snapping at God:

> You deceived me, LORD, and I was deceived;
> you overpowered me and prevailed. . . .
> The word of the LORD has brought me
> insult and reproach all day long. (Jer. 20:7–8 NIV)

While his complaint eventually ends in praise and surrender, it nevertheless begins with accusations of antagonism and broken promises. Jeremiah's grief not only for his own trials but also for the suffering of his people is one of his defining features. He is often referred to as "the weeping prophet," and his depiction on the Sistine Chapel ceiling reflects his exhaustion, his shoulders slumped and his head resting on one hand that partially covers his lined face. If Naomi is a model of action and agency, Jeremiah is a portrait of mourning.

Through Naomi and Jeremiah, we see believers who give voice to their frustrations with God. Rather than accept the world as it is, they unapologetically register their displeasure and take action in protest. Naomi's knowledge of the law (as well as human nature) allows her to formulate a plan to bring about changes in her family's situation. Jeremiah's protest comes in the form of artistic expression—namely, the aptly named book of Lamentations,

Although both Naomi and Jeremiah acknowledge the sovereignty of God, they do not also accept pain as their destiny.

which contains poetic cries for mercy and deliverance after the destruction of Jerusalem in 586 BCE. Although both Naomi and Jeremiah acknowledge the sovereignty of God, they do not also accept pain as their destiny. Neither did the family of Denise Mc-Nair and the other victims of the Birmingham church bombing, or their community at-large; by putting her blood-soaked belongings on display, they intentionally called attention to the fruits of evil rather than quietly surrendering so as to "keep the peace." What they, Naomi, and Jeremiah all show us is the spiritual discipline—and spiritual imperative—of defiance.

In fact, engaging with authority is at the very heart of Jesus's message in the Sermon on the Mount: "You have heard that it was said, 'An eye for an eye and a tooth for a tooth.' But I say to you, Do not resist an evildoer. But if anyone strikes you on the right cheek, turn the other also; and if anyone wants to sue you and take your coat, give your cloak as well; and if anyone forces you to go one mile, go also the second mile" (Matt. 5:38–41).

Though this passage has often been interpreted as a sign of Christian weakness or submission, in reality it is advocating something much more subversive. As many scholars have pointed out,[2] turning the other cheek does not have to mean letting an offense go; it can imply that the victim is still standing and refusing to back down; they may not hit back, but they are certainly not cowering. Similarly, giving someone your coat alongside your tunic wasn't quiet defiance; it communicated that you were hardy enough to weather the extremes of the environment. The same was true for going the extra mile. Roman soldiers could order villagers to carry their gear from one mile marker to the next one along the well-delineated Roman roads; it was a convenient way to remind the local populace of their feebleness next to Rome's military might. Carrying the equipment an *extra* mile, however, would communicate to the soldier, "I am strong enough to keep going. This doesn't faze me."

These are not orders to surrender to challenging circumstances; they are commands as to how we are to respond in strength.

These are not necessarily messages of combativeness, but neither are they messages of submission. Defiance in the face of injustice—against both others and ourselves—is not only to be tolerated but is to be celebrated. These are not orders to surrender to challenging circumstances; they are commands as to how we are to respond in strength. The Sermon on the Mount, after all, opens with a series of inversions: mourners will be comforted, the powerless will inherit, the hungry will be filled. When we find ourselves as victims, we do not somehow become better Christians by putting our heads down and keeping quiet. We are ordered to defy expectations and upend the status quo. We don't stay down when struck; we aren't so weak that we need extra protection; we demonstrate the strength to continue beyond the point expected of us. Jesus is not promoting acquiescence, *he is encouraging defiance.*

Paul understood this well. In Romans 12, he writes: "'If your enemies are hungry, feed them; if they are thirsty, give them something to drink; for by doing this you will heap burning coals on their heads.' Do not be overcome by evil, but overcome evil with good" (12:20–21). Heaping burning coals upon someone's head is hardly a gentle, passive image. Paul isn't telling his readers that Christians must always act sweetly; the verb translated "overcome" is a battle term that means literally to conquer or subdue. This isn't gentle persuasion, this is going to war with evil and overpowering it through the power of goodness.

We are called to call out the aggressors, the offenders, the harassers, and the oppressors. And we don't just do it on our own behalf: we name the corrupt, and we push back against those people and systems that victimize others. The defense of the powerless is, after all, one of the major themes running through the entire Bible. James writes, "Religion that is pure and undefiled before God, the Father, is this: to care for orphans and widows in their distress, and to keep oneself unstained by the world" (1:27). Deuteronomy 16:20 even packs a conditional blessing: "Follow justice and justice alone, so that you may live and possess the land the LORD your God is giving you" (NIV). The text clearly asserts that the fullness of God's gift is limited to those who pursue justice.

For the individual who does not understand why another person's experience or tragedy matters to us all, for the believer who is struggling with how to respond to situations of power-lessness or disappointment, we are called to push back against the very things that cause oppression and pain. God expects us to act. We *should* be angry about the unfairness and brokenness of the world, both on a personal and a social level, but we cannot fix what we do not see. When we call out injustice in any form, we not only make room for healing, but we become more fully realized versions of ourselves and of the body of Christ as a whole.

Too often, we are taught that anger is a "bad" emotion that faithful Christians should try to avoid. Jesus's confrontation with the money changers in the temple is held up as a notable exception to his otherwise peaceful persona. But this kind of aggressive action was not an isolated moment in his ministry. Jesus warns his disciples in Matthew 10: "Do not think that I have come to bring peace to the earth; I have not come to bring peace, but a sword" (10:34), and if the dressing down Jesus offers in Matthew 23 is any indication, raging about whitewashed tombs and broods of vipers, he certainly did not always speak to the Pharisees and Sadducees in calm, gentle tones.

> *When we call out injustice in any form, we not only make room for healing, but we become more fully realized versions of ourselves and of the body of Christ as a whole.*

Righteous anger is a sacred and beautiful thing. The mere fact that we are able to recognize something as unjust means that we also recognize that something else *is* just — that there is a better way, a separation between the way things are and the way we wish they were. When we witness hatred or suffering and react with frustration, we are inherently recognizing that something is broken; we can sense the disjunction from what we believe is God's will for all his people. The church, as the body of Christ, should always be looking for ways to bridge that gap, to "do justice, and to love kindness, and to walk humbly with [its] God" (Mic. 6:8). Our call to be like Christ is less about keeping the minutiae of the law or falling lockstep into the prevailing mode of religious thinking—Jesus left no question about where he stood on those matters—and more about bridging the gap between God and a hurting world. When we see situations that it seems a fair and loving God should not allow, we must act as Christ did, stepping in to provide whatever is needed, be it grace and mercy, or strength and influence, or allyship and solidarity. James 4:17 reminds us that the failure to act when we should carries the same guilt as violations we willingly commit: "Anyone, then, who knows the right thing to do and fails to do it, commits sin." Those Christians who willingly turn a blind eye to matters of injustice are engaging in gaslighting when they deny or discount someone else's lived experience simply because the fallout from those matters has never inconvenienced them.

Unfortunately, the Christian imperative to stand with the oppressed is often dismissed as "too political" or "unnecessarily divisive" by leaders who are comfortably situated in positions of power. Instead, they insist, it is more important to maintain unity within the congregation or fellowship of believers. Courtney, a freelance writer and mother of two, describes her frustration with this type of thinking:

> People love to talk about "unity." "Unity" means not challenging, not rocking the boat, not making the people in the pews uncomfortable. But Jesus's whole goal wasn't about keeping

people comfortable. He was constantly calling people out for not doing enough. Jesus did not come to flip the hierarchy; he came to do away with the hierarchy altogether. . . . A friend of mine was reprimanded by her church leadership recently for posting something on social media about how Christians in general need to be more socially involved. I think her response was perfect. She said: "'Can't the church do better?' should not be a controversial statement."

When we see things in the world that interrupt orderly justice or when we question why God would allow such suffering or brokenness to persist, we must remember that we do not have to accept things the way they are. Like a community that rallied around four murdered girls in Birmingham, we can refuse to back down. Like Naomi, we can take action to transform the circumstances around us. Even if there is absolutely nothing we can actively do to change the situation, we can cry out like Jeremiah instead of keeping silent. As the prophet declares:

> For whenever I speak, I must cry out,
>   I must shout, "Violence and destruction!"
> For the word of the LORD has become for me
>   a reproach and derision all day long.
> If I say, "I will not mention him,
>   or speak any more in his name,"
> then within me there is something like a burning fire
>   shut up in my bones;
> I am weary with holding it in,
>   and I cannot. (20:8–9)

If only we were all consumed by such a burning desire to cry out against violence and destruction. If only we all felt that raising our voices in protest to injustice was part of our religious imperative. "Can't the church do better?" should be our rallying cry. This kind of suffering is not evidence of heavenly anarchy, where God is somehow sleeping at the helm; it is God challenging *us* to be the peacemakers, the bringers of righteousness, the defenders of the innocent, the allies of the oppressed. This is the way that we become more like God. As Paul writes in Ephesians 4, "But speaking the truth in love, we must grow up in every way into him who is the head, into Christ" (4:15). *Speaking the truth*, not sweeping it under the rug or pretending we don't notice, is the very way we grow more like Christ.

Like Naomi and Jeremiah—like Jesus himself—we can show compassion. We can utilize our own abilities. We can fight. We can devise plans. We can create. We can speak up. We can cry out. We are not called to cower, to hide away, to bide our time hoping that things one day get better. We are not called to resign ourselves to the world as it is, accepting it as broken beyond repair. We are called to defy expectation—to shock those who would strike us by not backing down, to prove we are stronger and more powerful than they think.

If we confine the question of "What would Jesus do?" only to the slightly uncomfortable or mildly inconvenient questions of our own lives, we are missing the point entirely.

When we face evil in the world—real, visceral evil—we must have the courage to name it, to call attention to it, to lay it bare for all to see, whether that is by confronting it head-on or by putting a half-finished doll dress and a bloody Sunday school worksheet on display to make the consequences of evil impossible to ignore.

There is no silver lining to hatred and injustice; it is not enough to say, "Yes, but good came from it eventually." If we confine the question of "What would Jesus do?" only to the slightly uncomfortable or mildly inconvenient questions of our own lives, we are missing the point entirely. We know what Jesus would do: he would call people out, he would overturn tables, he would speak truth to power—even if it had no direct impact on his own life. Jesus gained nothing from his experience on the cross; that was all for the benefit of other people. And even in his resurrection, Jesus made clear that evil would not prevail; he would not allow it.

Neither should we.

12

ANXIETY AND ABUSE:
THE GOD OF MANIPULATION

> *Luke 18:9–14*
> *Matthew 22:34–40*

"E ven as a little kid, I realized that church was a game of falling in line," Stan explains to me over a Zoom call, his wife sitting beside him on the sofa while their kindergartner and rescue dog romp happily past the camera:

> You could ask questions as long as they stuck to the right script. And I could play the good church boy, so I learned what were the right questions to ask and not to ask, and I figured out how to be the star pupil.
>
> Everything changed in sixth grade when my former friends turned into bullies. I didn't know what to do; I would curl up in a ball and pray that they landed kicks where my parents couldn't see the bruises. I was doing everything by the book, so I knew everything that was supposed to happen. There might be a period of suffering, but David ultimately wins and Goliath falls. The bad guys get their comeuppance. That's how it works. I kept telling myself this would make a great story for my testimony when God finally intervened.

But I would pray and pray and pray and God did nothing. I finally came to the conclusion that God is either not who he says he is or else isn't nearly as powerful as people says he is and he can't help me—or else he wasn't there at all. But I knew he was there, so did he not love me or did he choose not to do anything about it? God was contractually obligated to love me because God is love, but there are others he loves more, and he must not be able to do anything for me.

And for a long time, that colored everything about how I saw myself and saw the world. My faith was a case of unrequited love. I wanted so desperately to be loved by God that I was doing all the right stuff in the desperate hopes that he would love me enough to help me. And then I started to wonder: If doing the "right" things mattered so much, did God ultimately love me or did he just love the formula?

Despite all the reassurances in Scripture of God's faithfulness and steadfast love, many of us struggle with wondering if we are worthy of God's attention and care, or if we are somehow below his notice and concern—especially when we are faced with struggles from which there seems to be no apparent delivery. The pastoral response to such anxiety usually falls into one of two camps: the goal is either to reassure struggling people that their fears are irrational due to God's unshakable mercy, or to chastise them by talking about "the sin of doubt." The first dismisses genuine and heartfelt concerns, and the second drives them into an even deeper state of anxiety; neither response acknowledges the validity of the emotions, which ultimately leads to gaslighting. When we deny people the reality of their experiences, we open the door for spiritual trauma.

In our rush to offer answers, we often forget to leave space simply to acknowledge the validity of individual concerns. It is almost as if we fear that the absence of a response is a sign of weakness, like an infinite God must be completely comprehensible or else we've somehow lost spiritual authority or footing. Such an approach not only reduces God to a few knowable facts but also writes off any uncertainty or complexity of emotion as either silly or sinful. In an effort to wipe away doubt, we run the risk of "taming" God, as C. S. Lewis might say—of making God soft and simple and easy to understand for our own convenience.

Such a tack may be well intentioned—no one operating from pure motives wants to see another believer in religious turmoil— but to dismiss this kind of anxiety out of hand is to deny people their lived experience of God, invalidating the way they engage with God or understand spiritual practice. Church leaders have the sacred responsibility of leading people to a better under-standing of God, but not in a way that invalidates the suffering party or makes the conflict worse. It is interesting, as well, that in Luke 18 Jesus tells the parable of a Pharisee and a tax collector praying together at the temple. Ultimately, it is not the confident man who Jesus says went home justified before God but the one who felt unworthy to be there (18:14). Sometimes our desire to "fix" a situation crowds out our compassion.

People with spiritual anxiety may experience any of the topics discussed in this book—feelings that God is angry with them, doesn't care, or has abandoned them. Ultimately, though, the root of their struggle is usually focused not on how God chooses to act (or refrain from acting), but on how their own thoughts and ac-tions connect them with God in tenuous, frightening, or distress-ing ways. Such fear may be related to general anxiety, but not always. Such spiritual anxiety often stems from condemnatory, demeaning, or abusive language employed in personal relation-ships or even from the pulpit, where the focus is fixed on human-ity's "unworthiness" of God's grace rather than the gift of grace itself—the weight of sin rather than the glory of forgiveness. In some cases, spiritual disquiet can also be tied to issues of mental health, such as obsessive-compulsive disorder, wherein sufferers struggle to release the obsession with their own imperfections or imperfect motives, thus trapping them in a state of perpetual guilt and desire for atonement through extra effort. The Roman Catholic Church even has a word for this kind of thinking, "scrupulosity," and sponsors theologians who are specially trained to help believers understand and navigate such challenging thought patterns in their own religious practice.[1] But, of course, some people are just natural worriers or pleasers, concerned with carrying out a task to the letter or ensuring that those around them approve of their efforts.

Whatever the case or cause, spiritual anxiety can be distressing and all-consuming for those who wrestle with feeling worthy of a relationship with God. Ava, whose struggles with doubt we discussed in chapter 8, offered this perspective on her spiritual anxiety:

> My dad or my preacher always tried to reassure me I was saved, but they can't know for sure. I know they meant well, but in my head I always heard that verse from Matthew repeating over and over: "Not everyone who says to me, 'Lord, Lord,' will enter the kingdom of heaven, but only the one who does the will of my Father in heaven. . . . Then I will say to them, 'Away from me, I never knew you'" [Matt. 7:21, 23]. And I wonder, "What is the qualifier there? What if I missed a box I was supposed to check?"

When people—including ourselves—struggle with spiritual anxiety, our job is not to explain it away but to hear them (or ourselves) out, to listen to their concerns, and to hold space for their struggle if we are able. Our job is not to "fix" their relationship with God by telling them that what they are feeling is wrong or broken, but to support and encourage them as they go through their own wrestling with the Lord.

Unfortunately, many people treat religion like a bandage they can slap onto someone else's situation to stop the bleeding and cover the wound, and consider it first aid—as if a human soul in turmoil is merely suffering from a sacred paper cut. Throwing memory verses at a problem does little long-term good if the source of that gaping wound of hurt, confusion, and fear is not also addressed. This is why trauma-informed ministry is so important, even though it is still struggling for recognition in many churches. Many leaders see anxiety as merely insufficient understanding of the Bible or willful rejection of the "joy of salvation" instead of recognizing that anxiety often stems from an impactful experience or painful background; in fact, even the impact of anxiety itself can be a kind of trauma. To explain away people's genuine concerns with a few verses communicates that their engagement with their faith is not valid or not complete—a message that merely confirms their fears that they are not good enough.

Unfortunately, many people treat religion like a bandage they can slap onto someone else's situation to stop the bleeding and cover the wound, and consider it first aid—as if a human soul in turmoil is merely suffering from a sacred paper cut.

As tempting as it may be to quote a list of classic "go-to" Scriptures about courage, joy, worry, and confidence—Joshua 1:9, Psalm 94:19, Jeremiah 17:7-8, Luke 12:22, and John 14:1, for example—it is important to frame such verses as general suggestions rather than commands or admonishments. For example, Philippians 4:6-7 may sound uplifting for persons without spiritual anxiety, but it can cause those who struggle with feeling worthy of connection to God to spiral because of the promise it carries: "Do not worry about anything, but in everything by prayer and supplication with thanksgiving let your requests be made known to God. And the peace of God, which surpasses all understanding, will guard your hearts and your minds in Christ Jesus." This is a helpful perspective and a good rule of thumb, but for people who have experienced a lasting trauma, or even those who are just naturally attuned to be planners or who have grave concerns about a situation, it's no simple task to simply let worries go. If transcendent peace does not seize their soul or quiet every fear, they may feel like a disappointment to God, which only adds to the anxiety and causes their feelings of failure to compound. This is made even worse when such guilt is coupled with conversations about eternal punishment intended to scare a person into a fear-based, "fire-insurance" repentance. Such emotions can lead to self-denigration of their own personhood or even eventually drive them to doubt God altogether.

All these concerns lead to the troubling issue of spiritual abuse, also called religious abuse or religious trauma, and it is here that spiritual gaslighting can be the most damaging because it directly impacts the way people perceive their relationship with God. That is certainly not to say that anxiety always stems from spiritual abuse, but the two very often go hand in hand. This type of abuse is a broad category generally classified as distress or damage done to an individual in the name of religion, for the sake of control, manipulation, or ideological dominance. It includes everything from sexual misconduct and abuse of power to psychological and mental manipulation through authoritarian systems that discourage dialogue or healthy questioning—and it is not limited to churches. While that is the most common place for spiritual abuse to happen, it can also occur in other faith-based organizations such as nonprofits, ministries, schools, or companies that claim to operate under "Christian principles"; it can even occur within personal relationships if religion is wielded as a means of manipulation or humiliation.

At the risk of oversimplifying, spiritual abuse has emerged as a hotly debated topic over the past thirty years as a result of the countless sex-abuse scandals that have roiled nearly every branch of Christianity and because of the physical harm and death that have resulted from so-called faith healings. Even more so, though, it has become a much more mainstream topic because of the psychological and emotional effects that often emerge

among members of authoritarian churches or because the prevailing theology of those churches can filter into society.

While the danger of this kind of conduct has been clear for
decades, for a long time it was generally considered the realm
of cults and zealots. Mainstream and evangelical churches were
largely considered immune to such abuses due to their compara-
tively loose control over their members' personal lives, especially
when compared to the brainwashing power of cults that captured
so many headlines in the 1960s and 1970s for their embrace of free
love, psychological drugs, and even heinous crimes. The insidious
nature of such groups made any missteps or problematic conduct
committed in the local church seem quite tame by comparison;
the local preacher might be controlling, but at least he didn't command his followers to commit mass suicide.

By the late 1980s, however, researchers were specifically examining the psychological effects of fear-based faith and religious control over members of groups that weren't as marginal, those often
existing on the fringe of more mainline denominations rather than
as their own separate movement or commune. The control executed
by such groups quickly emerged as "unnatural, unhealthy and dangerous" under professional evaluation,[2] and it was soon found to be
prevalent throughout every branch of Christianity, not just among
fundamentalist or ultra-traditional denominations. Psychologists
and mental health experts swiftly moved to classify such treatment
as abuse, with more than half a dozen books published on the subject between 1991 and 1993. Since then, the topic has only grown
in prevalence due in no small part to the widespread impact spiritual abuse has on the mental health and well-being of people who
have been shaped by it—both victims and perpetrators. It has, of
course, also been vociferously challenged by those who maintain
that such a classification is motivated by anti-Christian sentiments
to the point that it actually constitutes religious persecution (not to
mention ignored by many who consider it irrelevant or who eschew
academic research in general).

The fact remains, however, that there are measurable detrimental effects from following authoritarian theology that condemns those who fail to fall in lockstep with the dogmas of the denomination or prevailing cultural shibboleths. In our efforts to combat the notion of earned salvation, we have erased the significance of works. When our relationship with God rests solely on whether or not we believe exactly as the preacher demands, rather than on the way we meet the needs of the world or treat those within our own flock, the accountability of leadership is removed; in essence, such reductive faith removes any culpability for our actions, even—especially—when they harm people. No wonder people are leaving organized religion in droves; they are beginning to realize that Jesus can be seen more clearly in acts of love and inclusion than in messages of condemnation and rejection. For many, the prize of being counted as one of God's "in crowd" is no longer worth the weight of spiritual anxiety or the damage of spiritual abuse to themselves or others.

Even when it is possible to separate from an abusive religious environment, the impact is not automatically resolved by a break in relationship; in fact, the psychological trauma may even get worse for a time. One of the first articles published on spiritual abuse in fundamentalist churches focused on this very phenomenon, observing that people who leave such groups often battle "anxiety and depression . . . guilt, low self-esteem, sexual inhibitions, and vivid fears of divine punishment" even as they struggle with feelings of isolation and rejection by family and friends. The study notes:

> *For many, the prize of being counted as one of God's "in crowd" is no longer worth the weight of spiritual anxiety or the damage of spiritual abuse.*

> Ex-fundamentalists may continue to experience guilt for not living up to perfectionist standards. The most common type of guilt seems to be sexual, sometimes leading to dysfunction

or inhibition. Despite intellectually renouncing fundamentalist theology, some experience vivid fears of Hell or nagging
anxiety that somehow God will avenge their leaving. Finally,
fundamentalist methods and teachings may have reinforced
or contributed to the low self-esteem of former members. For
example, some fundamentalist groups publicly criticize and
humiliate those who deviate, emphasize that their members
would be "depraved" without God and their church, and subtly
encourage their members to "praise God" when things go well
and to blame themselves when things go wrong.[3]

This was exactly the experience faced by Courtney, whom we
met in chapter 11, and her husband, Mike, when he left the large
Christian company where he worked for nearly a decade. The organization placed its faith-based affiliation front and center as a
touchstone of its brand, all centered on a prominent charismatic
individual who was the face of the operation. During Mike's time
with the company, he and Courtney became aware of troubling
practices wrapped in the guise of Christianity, but they came to
experience spiritual abuse firsthand when Mike received a job offer
with a start-up in an unrelated field. "We thought he left on good
terms," Courtney tells me as we chat over Zoom roughly a year after
her husband's career change. "He voiced a few concerns in his exit
interview, but there were no hard feelings. Or so we thought."

In the months that followed, Mike's previous employer
reached out to his current one to disparage his character and
imply that the new company would be better off without him.
After sending people to their home with threatening letters, the
faith-based company met internally with current employees to
denigrate Mike's character and falsely accuse him of engaging in
malicious behavior, leading numerous people Mike considered
friends to abruptly cut all ties with him. As Courtney and Mike
tried to make sense of what was happening, they began to hear
similar stories from other former employees who had experi-

enced the same sort of harassment and character assassination. "Mike couldn't even defend himself," Courtney explains. "They had painted him as someone who gossiped and knew things he wasn't supposed to know, so he couldn't even reach out to former friends to explain that the allegations were untrue, because he wasn't supposed to even know those internal meetings had happened. Our best theory is that they must have been afraid he might know something damaging about them, so they set out to destroy him before he could say anything."

Rhetorically, the company had situated itself perfectly to win the PR battle. Because all discussion was so stringently forbidden, those who objected or voiced a concern to management simply confirmed their own untrustworthiness. And this, Courtney argues, is why spiritual abuse is so rampant:

A lot of these organizations are set up to facilitate abuse because it's baked into their doctrines. It's present in all of the systems of the organization. It's in how conflict resolution is handled, how disagreement is handled. There tends not to be an easy way to disagree because disagreement gets shut down. If you raise a concern to a leader or to the leadership team, it is seen as a spiritual failing: You don't trust enough. You are giving in to fear. You aren't trusting Jesus the way you're supposed to trust Jesus. You need to take a hard look at yourself to see why you would accuse good people. This is a heart issue with you.

If someone from outside the organization raises any sort of question, it gets painted as "We are under attack. This is spiritual warfare and Satan is after us, which means we have to be doing something right. They want to see us fail, but God is on our side. Don't you want to be on God's side?"

Which means that if you are on the inside hearing this, even if you have felt that certain things aren't right, if you agree with what the other person said, you are siding with Satan, you are siding with the evil people. The Enemy is attacking you. It always gets turned back around to what is wrong with you.

They set it up so they couldn't fail. They said: "If we are doing really well, it's because God is blessing us—it's God's favor upon us. We are doing something right so God is blessing us with abundance. But if we are being attacked, then it's also God's favor because it means that Satan wants to bring us down." . . .

The conversation was always "This is God's plan for this topic" not "This is my understanding or interpretation of God's plan for this topic." So if you didn't agree with it, you were against God.

Courtney grew up in a denomination that took a similarly authoritarian approach to faith, and through the ordeal with her husband's former employer, the family sought counseling to help them make sense of it all and deal with the emotional toll it was taking. In these discussions, Courtney found herself having flashbacks to her own childhood:

Any time I raised a question or said something didn't sound right—and I learned early not to do that—I was told, "You just need to trust more. These men (it was always men) have been ordained by God. It is not up to you to question them." . . .

A common factor I've found in all these environments that I would classify as spiritually abusive is that any questions or disagreements or doubt are always turned around as a moral failing on the part of the questioner. It's presented as "The only people who ask questions are bad people who want to see us fail." . . .

Mike reached out to HR during the rise of the #MeToo movement to see what procedures were in places for reporting sexual misconduct, and the head of HR told him, "We don't have means of reporting it because that wouldn't happen here because we are a Christian organization." They added that they wouldn't do any training, either, "because that would make us look bad because people would think we had issues going on here that we don't." . . .

This isn't a bug, it's a feature. It's not just a matter of "Let's root out the abuses in the system by the ones who have been the most vile and the most cocky on such a large scale." It's not just them. So many people do it on a small scale in the church down the street or the small "Christian" business. It's not unique to a handful of bad, charismatic leaders. It's systemic. First, the system rewards that kind of behavior and, as a result, other people are drawn to it. And secondly, it becomes so normalized that otherwise good people start engaging in these traits, in these abusive tactics, because that's what they see modeled.

Abuse in the name of faith is still abuse. It's not somehow less serious because it is done under the guise of religious zeal; if anything, that makes it even worse because, when challenged, the perpetrators can retreat behind their platitudes of righteousness or insist that "These are God's words, not mine" and thus evade any personal responsibility for the harm they have done or the injury inflicted in the name of their faith. They have no recourse for their actions because anyone who questions them is simply cast as an enemy working against God's people. And so, armed with the self-appointed authority of God, they are free to build empires and declare themselves specially anointed, free to wield power unchecked and unchallenged. If the old saying is true that power corrupts and absolute power corrupts absolutely, it's no wonder that abuse thrives in such environments.

The rhetoric in spiritually abusive organizations is often rooted in a type of logical fallacy called an appeal to ignorance—that is, the claims of authority are rooted in something that is unprovable. In the case of religious manipulation, it almost always takes the form of claiming God's favor or a privileged position of "rightness" within the sacred framework. As Courtney pointed out, the definition of "God's favor" can be twisted to whatever interpretation best fits the current circumstances or agenda of those in power. They literally cannot lose. And when people in power believe their own logical fallacies, they see themselves as handpicked by God to be among the elite few who have solved the mystery of salvation.

"The ministry [of Mike's former employer] is based on the idea that we want to be winners. It's all about 'winning' at life and being different from the people around you," Courtney shares.

> But in order for there to be winners, there have to be losers. The language is all about how to be among the select few at the loss of the majority. That's essential to their message because if the tables are turned and there are more winners than losers, then I'm not special. They say they want to change the world, but they don't actually support larger policies that would support that because their whole model is built on exclusivity. "If God's kingdom is bigger than I think it is, bigger than this particular reading of Scripture or these specific steps of behavior, then I'm not special anymore."

Any one of us can probably name half a dozen specific examples: heads of ministries who harassed and assaulted women for years; pedophiles who strike again after being allowed back in local congregations because "God has forgiven them; why can't you?"; televangelists who defraud their followers to fund lavish lifestyles; preachers who spew hate from the pulpit; institutions that made bigotry part of their core beliefs for years (and still do); family members who wield religious guilt as a means of control. They have all weaponized God. They are all guilty of bastardizing grace. They have all injured other souls while hiding behind a mask of holiness.

As victims of assault, injustice, and oppression are giving voice to their stories like never before, it is time that people of faith feel permission to do the same. Victimhood, as a concept, has been vilified by society, which tends to cast people claiming it either as powerless, passive doormats or as overly sensitive complainers who crave pity, special favors, or an absolution of responsibility for the results of their actions. The problem with such an attitude is that many people are so dedicated to avoiding the victim mindset that they fail to recognize that they are being victimized at all. It is gaslighting in its purest form.

It is time to reclaim victimhood. We must allow survivors of spiritual abuse—whether physical, psychological, or emotional—to be heard, to tell their stories, to express their pain, to give voice to their betrayal. We must be willing to call out perpetrators, to name their crimes and share the evidence of their abuses, rather than hush, subdue, or otherwise stifle these stories in the name of protecting Christianity's reputation. Christianity's reputation has already been damaged not only by these insidious actions but also by the cover-up, rationalization, or disparaging of the whistleblowers that seems inevitably to follow. We aren't doing any favors to the institution when we ignore, justify, or cover up spiritual abuse; in fact, when we do so, we become complicit in the abuse ourselves. When churches rely on the empty maxim, "People aren't infallible," what they are really saying is, "We don't want to do the uncomfortable work of addressing this or holding people accountable." What's more, spiritual abuse cannot be explained away as a simple lapse of good judgment; it is an intentional and deliberate means to establish and maintain power. Just as no one "inadvertently" beats their child or "accidentally" verbally denigrates their spouse, spiritual abuse does not happen without a toxic system already in place. The abusers are simply utilizing faith as their weapon of choice. When we excuse abuse with a shrug, we are telling victims, "You don't matter enough for us to hold people

> *Many people are so dedicated to avoiding the victim mindset that they fail to recognize that they are being victimized at all.*

to basic standards of decency." And judging from the anxiety and feelings of rejection or unworthiness that are so common among people within Christian churches, this message has been received loud and clear.

The challenge, of course, is how to help people with spiritual anxiety and survivors of spiritual abuse to recognize and acknowledge their own worth. How do we support those on the road to healing? How do we take the first cautious steps toward claiming our birthright as valued and cherished children of God when it has been stripped from us? First, we separate ourselves from our abusers as much as possible. We seek help from vetted and certified counselors who will not cause retraumatization with more damaging theology. We extend grace when old thoughts and patterns creep in. But most of all, we recognize that we are deserving of love. If this sounds overly simplistic, that's because it is. Spiritual anxiety and abuse may never fully resolve; the fear may never be completely replaced with peace, and the emotional scars may never disappear. But the first step toward any kind of change must be a recognition of our own inherent worth.

Stan, whose story opened this chapter, explains how he came to terms with his own spiritual anxiety, his eyes tearing up as he leans into the camera on his laptop:

> Body, soul, spirit. This is what I've been given to make a connection to the divine. If I don't love the vessel, it's like pouring water into a cup a foot to the left. A few drops may get in, but the cup isn't filled. I'm not drowning in the love. I never thought that learning to love myself was part of the logical development of how to love God. That wasn't anything I was taught growing up.
>
> I can love my enemy easily simply by looking at them and forcing myself to recognize that they are an image-bearer of God. I can love my neighbor that way, too. But the hardest part is looking into the mirror and recognizing that I am an image-

bearer, too. I am worth loving. I'm not perfect, but even if all the things I hold to technically are wrong, I have enough faith, have experienced enough, lost enough to know that what I am holding onto is love. . . . If I get everything else wrong, at least I know I loved well, and Jesus said that was how you would know his followers.

We love well. We love through our pain or anxiety. We love ourselves despite what our spiritual abuse may have told us about how unlovable we are. We project it outward toward the world and we project it inward, at our own souls, which are every bit as "fearfully and wonderfully made" as anyone else in creation (Ps. 139:14). If you find yourself struggling with spiritual anxiety or the effects of spiritual abuse, consider whether they stem from a fear-based gospel centered on repression and punishment rather than love and acceptance.

Philippians 2:4 tells us, "Let each of you look not only to his own interests, but also to the interests of others" (ESV), but there is some variation among translations in how to accurately transcribe the word *kai*, which appears in the final phrase. *Kai* is a conjunction, a word that connects clauses or words within a sentence, such as "and," "but," or "so." Interestingly, it appears more than nine thousand times in the New Testament, usually translated as "and" or "also" or even, in some cases, going untranslated altogether depending on the grammar of the translation. In this case, many translators maintain that *kai* functions as a correlative conjunction like the word "also," which is how many translations render it, so that the verse reads as rendered above: "Let each of you look *not just* to your own interests, but *also* to the interests of others." Other translators leave the word untranslated, rendering the verse along the lines of "Let each of you look *not* to your own interests, but to the interests of others." Notice the difference: the second translation reads as if the needs of others are the only things that matter, whereas the first version takes as given that the reader will be looking after their own needs and the concerns of others are simply to be added to that.

The rule in such instances where shades of meaning may exist is to allow context to guide translation. In other words, which translation is the most consistent with the rest of the passage? In this case, many translators agree that the first reading acknowledges the necessity of caring for ourselves and valuing our own needs and concerns rather than automatically subjugating them to the needs of others. In fact, Paul writes in the same passage, this is the way to "make my joy complete: be of the same mind, having the same love, being in full accord and of one mind" (Phil. 2:2). The grace and compassion we extend to others in the name of Christ, we ought to extend to ourselves, too, as part of a healthy faith community. This may not relieve spiritual anxiety, but it does grant us the freedom to be kind to ourselves as well as to others who may be struggling with the issue.

How can we allow the context of Jesus's teachings—not a preacher in a pulpit or an armchair theologian, but the literal incarnate God—to serve as an example to guide the interpretation of our lives?

But even if the Bible did not extend such permission, what would we believe about offering love and acting in gentleness toward ourselves? Would we believe we are wretched worms unworthy of a backward glance from God or vile creatures the Creator regrets creating? Or would we believe that we are valuable and complex creations that are worthy of love and dignity? Which interpretation is more consistent with Christ's example? How can we allow the context of Jesus's teachings—not a preacher in a pulpit or an armchair theologian, but the literal incarnate God—to serve as an example to guide the interpretation of our lives?

Similarly, we must consider how Jesus would respond to spiritual abuse—to twisted teachings and traumas committed in his name. We already know how he responded to the Sadducees and

Pharisees—men more committed to the letter of the law than the spirit of it. He did not mince words when he accused them of duplicity, exclusion, and corrupting the whole idea of God to their own twisted notions: "But woe to you, scribes and Pharisees, hypocrites! For you lock people out of the kingdom of heaven. For you do not go in yourselves, and when others are going in, you stop them. Woe to you, scribes and Pharisees, hypocrites! For you cross sea and land to make a single convert, and you make the new convert twice as much a child of hell as yourselves" (Matt. 23:13–15).

Yet Jesus simultaneously shows compassion to hurting souls. Just a few verses before that damning statement against the religious leaders of his day, Jesus answers frankly when asked which of the laws was most important: "'You shall love the Lord your God with all your heart, and with all your soul, and with all your mind.' This is the greatest and first commandment. And a second is like it: 'You shall love your neighbor as yourself.' On these two commandments hang all the law and the prophets" (Matt. 22:37–40). Loving our neighbor is not secondary to loving God; it is not what happens after we finish our devotions and personal Bible study. The second command Jesus cites is literally said to be "like" the first; the word in Greek means "same." Loving our neighbors is on the same footing as loving God. They are one and the same, of equal importance. Loving our neighbors is *how* we love God. As Matthew records just three chapters later, Jesus explains how feeding the poor and caring for the sick is the same as doing it for God: "And the king will answer them: 'Truly I tell you, just as you did it to one of the least of these who are members of my family, you did it to me'" (25:40). Nowhere does Jesus teach that we love God by alienating or traumatizing our neighbor.

> *Loving our neighbors is on the same footing as loving God.*

But Jesus goes on: "Love your neighbor as yourself." Loving yourself is part of the command. Love yourself enough to recognize your inherent worth. Love yourself enough to walk away from abuse. Love yourself enough to seek help. Love yourself enough to set boundaries. Love yourself enough to enforce them as best you can. Love yourself when old scars and traumas—the sins of others—still impact your life. Love others enough to speak up in an effort to spare anyone else from being traumatized at the hands of spiritual abusers. And love yourself enough to protect your own mental health if you don't feel ready to speak up.

Your humanity is worth more to God than a spiritual checklist.

The cornerstone of Christ's example was elevating humanity over dogma. That hasn't changed; your humanity is worth more to God than a spiritual checklist. Sit with that truth as long as it takes. Remind yourself of it as often as you need to. When you believe it enough to act on it, you will be taking your first steps toward peace, safety, and freedom.

13

ALLEGORY:
THE GOD WHO MUST FIT OUR NARRATIVE

Mark 8:1–33

I met Felicity more than twenty years ago, when she was the first person to invite me into the social life of the church in the city to which I had just moved for graduate school. As I learned more about her traumatic past—incest leading to pregnancy and an abortion at thirteen—I witnessed how she struggled with feeling continually rejected: first by her biological family, who disavowed her when she spoke up about her abuse; next by her local church, who condemned her abortion; then, years later, by another church that took the general view that she needed to finally "get over" the trauma of her past; and finally, by the family that had informally adopted her as a teenager when she came out as a gay adult.

"People love to tell you, 'Everything happens for a reason,' but you can't say that to people who have lived with abuse," Felicity explains to me over a Zoom call one winter afternoon, the sky visibly darkening while we talk.

Just saying that is another kind of abuse because it implies that what happened to them is okay because it somehow serves a greater purpose. . . . I was told that the reason I was still struggling as an adult was because there was still sin in my life since I couldn't forgive my mother and stepfather. My stepfather began raping me when I was three and my mother called me a "prostitute" when I finally told her about it when I got older. That is not deserving of honor, and I don't believe I'm sinning if I'm still angry over what that did to me and to my life. There are some things we shouldn't be willing to overlook. I'm not going to try to find some silver lining in what my parents did.

* * *

There is an expression in writing circles that "the ending should be inevitable but not predictable"; in other words, let it surprise the audience, but upon reflection, they should be able to recognize all the elements feeding into that ultimate outcome as the best and most satisfying conclusion. Every part of the story should carry some weight in the narrative and impact the final outcome.

The ending makes or breaks every great narrative, and our trials are no different. As we discussed in chapter 12, creating order out of chaos is the basis of nearly every story ever told. It's the story of Genesis: light separated from darkness, firmament from terra firma. It is the story of the cross: redemption that conquers the chaos of sin. It is the story of every life: finding meaning in the midst of pain and suffering. Meaning making is an inherently human trait; horses don't seek out metaphorical applications of anecdotes and birds don't engage in philosophy. In Genesis 2:19–20, Adam names the animals in an act that helps assert and affirm his primacy among the created beings. It is as if the text is reminding us from the beginning that the act of creating order and imposing it on the world is part of what separates people from beasts.

In fact, the human brain craves order to the point that it will often create connections between unrelated events, a behavior called apophenia, or even fabricate meaning from random stimuli, such as hearing strains of music in white noise or seeing shapes in the clouds, a type of apophenia called pareidolia. The phenomenon is related to confirmation bias, where we give credence only to the facts that make sense to us or support the outcome we desire and ignore the rest. In *A Midsummer Night's Dream*, Shakespeare even refers to the pairing of confirmation bias and pareidolia as Theseus describes the universal human tendency to see what we want to see or scare ourselves with harmless objects:

> Such tricks hath strong imagination,
> That if it would but apprehend some joy,
> It comprehends some bringer of that joy.
> Or in the night, imagining some fear,
> How easy is a bush supposed a bear. (5.1.18–22)

While this kind of thinking is an unconscious trick or prejudice of the brain, we may also apply the principles of apophenia much more deliberately to make meaning during a chaotic season of life. When faced with a tragedy or series of disruptive events that seem completely inexplicable—unjust, illogical, or seemingly inconsistent with the acts of a loving Savior—we often rush to "find God" in the situation. We may search for symbolism in every little thing or even look ahead to the ending, determined to parse out God's will to assign meaning to the mayhem. We might try to guess where the ultimate story may be headed by saying things like, "But maybe *this* is happening now so *that* can happen later." Maybe we remind ourselves of Philemon 15-16: "Perhaps this is the reason he was separated from you for a while, so that you might have him back forever, no longer as a slave but more than a slave, a beloved brother." We cling to Romans 8:28 like a

lifeline, reciting the words "We know that all things work together for good for those who love God, who are called according
to his purpose" until they become a kind of sacred chant or even
a talisman to ward away any feelings of doubt, disappointment,
or disillusionment. We work so hard to find meaning that we
sometimes begin to assign significance to our struggles that may
or may not be God's intention for them. In short, we turn the
realities of our life into a kind of Christian allegory, in which each
character, location, and event has a symbolic function to further
the central moral of the story.

The Pilgrim's Progress, perhaps the best-known allegory in the
English language, tells the story of a man named Christian as
he makes his way from the City of
Destruction to the Celestial City
while facing detours and temp-
tations from such destinations as
the Slough of Despair and Vanity
Fair. Carrying a heavy burden that
finally drops from his back at "the
place of deliverance," he must still
face obstacles including the Hill of Difficulty and the Valley of
the Shadow of Death while engaging with a cast of characters
bearing such names as Sloth, Presumption, Faithful, and Hopeful.
Written by Puritan preacher John Bunyan while he was imprisoned in 1678, The Pilgrim's Progress was eventually expanded and
translated into more than two hundred languages. For much of
the eighteenth and nineteenth centuries, it was the second-most-
printed book in the world, surpassed only by the Bible itself.

It's no wonder, then, that this story influenced the way modern Christian theology tends to frame faith as a journey fraught
with symbolism. The allegory of The Pilgrim's Progress shaped the
way generations of theologians understood the Christian walk,
even serving as part of the narrative arc for such classic secular
novels as Louisa May Alcott's Little Women and the subtitle for

> We work so hard to find meaning
> that we sometimes begin to as-
> sign significance to our struggles
> that may or may not be God's
> intention for them.

Charles Dickens's *Oliver Twist: The Parish Boy's Progress*. The reach of Bunyan's book was so pervasive, at least in part, because the allegory does the heavy lifting of assigning and developing the symbolism and transparent meaning to the story—the kind of clear significance and signaling we naturally crave in the midst of the esoteric struggles of human life.

Of course, symbolism has been part of the Christian faith since its very beginning. From the parables Jesus used for teaching to the bread and the wine of communion, from the secret signs of the early church persecuted under Roman rule to the coded representations of the saints in medieval iconography for illiterate parishioners, metaphorical representations have always been an important way that believers interact with and understand their religion. Symbols are a highly effective tool for making difficult or esoteric concepts more relatable; the problem is that we can sometimes become so steeped in symbolic thinking around our beliefs that we become obsessed with finding deeper meaning in *everything*. When we become obsessed with trying to suss out "What God is trying to tell us," we may reach the point that we put our faith in the metaphor or the symbol itself, rather than in God.

When we become obsessed with trying to suss out "What God is trying to tell us," we may reach the point that we put our faith in the metaphor or the symbol itself, rather than in God.

As a result, we may bend our interpretation of occurrences and outcomes to fall in line with a pre-fabricated image of what we imagine our story's final outcome is supposed to be. In effect, we manipulate our perceptions and reactions in the direction of an artificially determined conclusion, rather than letting the events run their natural course. Allegory is fiction—a curated story in which the writer is in control of all characters and events, steering them toward their predetermined outcomes; real life obviously does not operate that way. And yet, it is difficult to resist the urge to assign significance to the sequence of certain events. The promise of a satisfying ending makes the trials themselves more bearable.

Interestingly, we can trace our obsession with outcomes-as-ending all the way back to a cultural clash that was happening at the time Jesus was teaching. Since the late fourth century BCE, the territory of ancient Israel had been occupied by troops, first from Greece and later from Rome. Naturally, the conquerors brought with them their traditions and beliefs, which they imposed upon the nations they ruled in a process called hellenization, wherein cultural notions from Greece were absorbed into the local customs. Among the opposing worldviews between the Jewish people and their hellenizing colonizers was the way each group understood the passage of time.

The Greek view, which was held by the ruling political class and subsequently shaped the modern Western understanding of time as well, was that of humanity traveling *forward* into the future, with our faces toward the unknown as we move ahead, more or less in a straight line, toward one ultimate ending. This contrasts sharply with the Jewish understanding of time, which saw the process in reverse.

If you imagine a boat, the ancient Greeks saw themselves as standing at the bow, looking in the direction the boat was moving. The Jewish people, on the other hand, saw themselves more like the rowers, facing the opposite direction. They move forward with their backs to the future and their faces toward the past, because we can really only understand the future by observing and analyzing what has come before, which sometimes involves circling back as one idea builds on another.[1] In fact, in Biblical Hebrew, words for "yesterday" and "tomorrow" are related to the words meaning "in front" or "behind/in back," respectively. The idea is that we move through time by observing what we have already experienced. The future is behind us because it is unknowable; we cannot see it until it has passed us—and it does so cyclically rather than linearly, so that the path of history is more like a corkscrew than a straight line. The Greek view of time became the dominant perception in the West, and as a result, it has influenced the way life and faith are often discussed in Western Christianity.

It is one thing to view the development of our faith as a walk; it's another thing to view it as a journey with an end goal that we must reach or risk failing in the entire endeavor. When we view the progress of our faith as a bold push into the unknown rather than as a thoughtful examination of our experiences, we leave ourselves guessing at the outcome; the problem with this approach is that we may begin to interpret the facts in accordance with our best guesses or confirmation bias. As a result, we often end up reading our will onto God's as we try desperately to guess the divine meaning.

It can feel like our Christian duty to look for God's will in the midst of tragedy, but we run the risk of oversimplifying our pain, or the pain of others, when we reduce a tragedy to its (often tangential) aftereffects. Even worse, we can inadvertently imply that the end was worth the means, no matter how appalling, or even that God orchestrated terrible events to happen for an outcome that serves our own purpose.

> *We often end up reading our will onto God's as we try desperately to guess the divine meaning.*

When Sam lost his beloved wife, Carole, to complications from multiple sclerosis, the entire extended family was devastated. Impacted by this tragedy, one of Sam's nieces decided life was too short to stay in a career field she hated, so she left her corporate job to begin working for a nonprofit. At a family reunion a decade later, she approached Sam and, in the course of the conversation, remarked: "Just think! If Aunt Carole hadn't died, I never would have found my true calling. God works in mysterious ways."

"What am I supposed to do with that?" Sam asks, the sting of the comment clearly still needling him several years later. Leaning back in his chair, fading photos of Carole with their boys visible on the wall behind him, he shrugs. "Am I supposed to rejoice that my children grew up without their mother because you needed a career change? Are you saying my wife dying was part of God's plan to land you your dream job? I know [my niece] didn't mean to be insensitive, but we've got to be really, really careful about how quick we are to classify things as 'God's will' without considering what else that implies."

In Mark 8, we see a virtual comedy of errors as Jesus confounds his disciples' expectations over and over again. First, he produces a meal to feed four thousand from the seven small loaves and a few fishes the disciples offer (8:5-8). Then, the Pharisees press Jesus for a "sign from heaven"—a request about which he "sighed deeply in his spirit" before declining (8:12). Immediately afterward, Jesus warns his disciples against the metaphorical yeast of Herod and the Pharisees, but the disciples take him literally and believe he is chastising them for forgetting to pack more bread (8:14-16). Later in the chapter, Jesus asks his disciples who the crowds say he is, then asks again who *they* think he may be (8:27-29). Finally, as Jesus tells of the "great suffering" he must endure before being killed and rising again, Peter scolds him and tells him to stop such talk. At this point, Jesus speaks his famous line, chastising Peter for speaking on matters he does not understand: "Get behind me, Satan! For you are setting your mind not on divine things but on human things" (8:33). Throughout this chapter, we see incident after incident of Jesus showing up differently than assumed. Sometimes he does more than expected, like feeding the crowd; sometimes he does less than expected, like refusing to produce a sign; sometimes he is misunderstood or even corrected in his own teaching by one of his closest followers. It is almost as if these stories were intentionally grouped together by Mark for maximum impact on the audience.

Perhaps the most striking example of this thematic grouping is the strange little story that appears in the midst of these other arguments about bread, yeast, and a messianic agenda. Almost as an aside during these other discussions, the text tells us that Jesus stopped to cure a blind man in Bethsaida. This interaction differs from his other miracles, however, in that the restoration of the man's sight is not perfect on the first attempt. After Jesus applies saliva to the blind man's eyes, he asks the patient: "'Can you see anything?' And the man looked up and said, 'I can see people, but they look like trees, walking.' Then Jesus laid his hands on his eyes again; and he looked intently and his sight was restored, and he saw everything clearly" (8:22–26).

It is no coincidence that, in the middle of a series of stories about people misreading everything about what Jesus is doing, we find someone who interacted with Jesus but literally could not see reality clearly on his first attempt. Rhetorically, this story of healing reinforces exactly what Jesus was facing at the time among both his followers and enemies: an unfocused and inaccurate understanding of what was actually unfolding around them. With their limited vision, both the disciples and the Pharisees (as well as the blind man of Bethsaida) interpreted what they saw. Sometimes Jesus corrected their misunderstanding; other times, he let it go. But every time, there was some degree of disappointment or confusion when Jesus failed to produce the results or act in the way they seemed to think he should.

Our understanding of what the outcome "should" be is rarely as accurate or as complete as God's. We often bring to the story our own biases of the direction we think the story ought to take and make choices accordingly. We like to imagine that, ultimately, every struggle and every heartache will prove part of a beautiful and deeply satisfying outcome, just like a well-crafted novel. We tell ourselves that God is the ultimate Writer of the ultimate story, and if we just trust in him, everything will work out neatly in the end. After all, the traditional translation of Hebrews 12:2 refers to Jesus as "the author and perfecter of our faith."

Unfortunately, this language is a misinterpretation of the original Greek. The word traditionally translated as "author"

comes from the root word *archē*, meaning the first or primary of
something. (This is where we get the English word "archetype,"
meaning the model upon which all others are based.) Its literal
meaning is "originator" or "founding leader" of a line of succes-
sion or movement; in fact, many modern translations such as the
NIV and NRSV now use the word "pioneer" rather than "author,"
rendering the passage as "Jesus the pioneer and perfecter of our
faith." This translation may just seem to indicate a minor seman-
tic difference, but the implications are actually quite significant:
"pioneer" indicates that Jesus founded the faith by setting it in
motion, not that he crafted every detail of the way it unfolds in
our lives the way an author would. Also, the word translated "perfecter" in most translations of Hebrew 12:2 applies to what Jesus
does within the faith itself, not what happens to our personal
stories. In other words, it is not our lives but *the grace of God in
our lives* that reflects perfection. And here again we see the Greek
concept of time present in New Testament thought: there is a
pioneering moment—a beginning—as well as a terminus, when
the action has been completed to perfection. But our faith is not
always a straight path toward the finish line.

Despite our best efforts, a neat resolution is not always in
the cards. Sometimes you do everything you're supposed to—
read all the books, go to counseling, work on communication
and forgiveness—and the marriage still fails. Sometimes you do
everything right—no caffeine, no hot baths, no parabens—and
the pregnancy miscarries anyway. Sometimes you follow the
doctor's orders—exercise regularly, eat an organic diet, endure
every chemo treatment—and the cancer still progresses. You
do everything the perpetrator demands—you are compliant,
you don't speak out—and yet the abuse continues. You're left
wondering what story is made better in the end by a broken
family or a dead baby or a relentless tumor or an exploited
child, and what kind of God would write such a narrative in
the first place?

Job 42 tells us, "The LORD blessed the latter part of Job's life more than the former part. He had fourteen thousand sheep, six thousand camels, a thousand yoke of oxen and a thousand donkeys. And he also had seven sons and three daughters" (42:12–13 NIV). It's a happy ending to a story full of pain and loss. But would we still hold the book in the same regard if we didn't have the last chapter? What if we never got to see the redemption? Restoration was never promised to Job. He didn't cling to his faith because he believed God would make it up to him in the end. The book *should* lose none of its impact if the recovering of Job's fortunes is left out, but how deeply dissatisfying the trials would seem without the payoff. How empty and meaningless Job's suffering would feel to us if order never emerged from the chaos. And yet, how often this emptiness colors our own lives when there is no apparent redemption arc.

Perhaps we turn to Joel 2:25 for comfort, applying God's promise to Israel to ourselves, that "I will repay you for the years that the swarming locust has eaten"—and we wait, year after year, for restoration, but the repayment seems to be stuck in arrears. The trauma continues to impact us; the pain persists. We continue, for decades, to pay the price for injuries we suffered or crimes committed against us. The effects can reverberate throughout every aspect of our lives. It's not that our faith is conditional or transactional, causing us to grow frustrated with God because he declined to tie up our story with a neat bow or to bring us the resolution we believed we deserved. It's recognizing that we were denied the basic safety and well-being that should be our birthright. This isn't mere disappointment that the ending failed to play out as expected; this is a denial of fundamental human necessities. When people insist that life-changing, soul-crushing hurt will somehow all be worth it, or that we will one day be glad of what we went through because of what came of it, they are (as we discussed in chapter 4) putting their faith in the outcome rather than in God.

C. S. Lewis once wrote that Matthew 24:34 was "the most embarrassing verse in the Bible."[2] In that Scripture, Jesus promises
that the second coming is imminent, declaring, "Truly I tell you,
this generation will not pass away until all these things have
taken place." Of course, as we all know, things did not go down
exactly as Jesus seems to have anticipated. We are still here, some
two millennia later, and he has not yet returned. Even Jesus seems
to have been operating from a set of assumptions and outcomes
to which God the Parent felt no obligation. But, as Lewis points
out, exactly one sentence later Jesus adds, "But about that day and
hour no one knows, neither the angels of heaven, nor the Son,
but only the Father" (24:36). Clearly, the story didn't play out the
way Jesus imagined it, nor most of the earliest Christians, who
seemed quite confident that their deliverance was imminent. As
time went by and those believers died off one by one without the
realization of their hopes and expectations, how did they feel?
At some point, each of them had to make a decision, as the Lord's
return continued to elude them: Were they going to continue to
put their faith in an outcome they may have misunderstood and
may never see, or were they going to put their faith in God while
doing their best to make meaning in their present lives?

What about us? Are we forging face-forward into the future,
determined to assign names and values to shapes we can barely
make out? Are we guessing at the future, declaring ourselves vi-
sionaries and then blaming God when things don't play out the
way we said they would or fearing we will derail the entire heavenly plan if we guess wrong? Or are we willing to keep rowing,
to accept our story as it unfolds, examining it as we live it and
discerning its significance in relation to what has already passed?
In short, does it depend on *our* knowing or *God's* knowing?

In Daniel 3, Shadrach, Meshach, and Abednego famously testify to the king of Babylon that their God will save them from the
fiery furnace: "*But even if he does not*, we want you to know, Your

Majesty, that we will not serve your gods or worship the image of gold you have set up" (v. 18 NIV). In Hebrews 11, the famous "faith chapter," the writer describes other believers who suffered a very different outcome than the one they probably wanted:

> Others suffered mocking and flogging, and even chains and imprisonment. They were stoned to death, they were sawn in two, they were killed by the sword; they went about in skins of sheep and goats, destitute, persecuted, tormented—of whom the world was not worthy. They wandered in deserts and mountains, and in caves and holes in the ground.
>
> Yet all these, though they were commended for their faith, did not receive what was promised, since God had provided something better so that they would not, apart from us, be made perfect. (11:36-40)

What we often forget is that we are never guaranteed answers, let alone a satisfying ending in this lifetime. Sometimes we are left only with a divine promise that suffering sanctifies and order really does conquer chaos. We think that the outcome conquers all, so we tend to skip over the parts of the story that make us uncomfortable or for which we don't have answers because we've been taught all our lives that "Jesus is the answer"—even if the question is something else entirely. We demand to know *why* without stopping to acknowledge that this is often the most difficult question for anyone to answer.

We've been taught all our lives that "Jesus is the answer"—even if the question is something else entirely.

When children are small, they are often satisfied with the simple, honest response of "because God made it that way." But as they get older, the *whys* are rooted less in curiosity about facts about the world and more in posing a challenge. "Why are those the rules?" or "Why is that the way the world works?" Suddenly, the trusty standby response "because God made it that way" is no longer enough. People who have endured real struggles and engaged with real spiritual wrestling know "because God made it that way" will not satisfy a hurting soul that recognizes the disconnect between the world as it should be and the world as it is. We want to know the reasons behind the struggle. We want to know what God is thinking and what God is planning, and we feel cheated when those answers are not supplied to us.

How do we persist when there is no reason offered or no meaning sufficient to account for the pain? How do we keep going when we have no way of knowing what our part in God's plan might be, and whether our struggles are a sign we are in the will of God or outside of it—or whether there is any will at all? Sacred suffering is often celebrated as an ideal—a sign that we, as believers, are taking a hard line against sin and temptation; the more we suffer, the greater our sanctification. But a struggle without reason just feels empty or even cruel.

When we endure difficult trials with no apparent redeeming endgame, we often receive well-meaning encouragement about the "refiner's fire" that will strengthen our character. But metal is scorching hot when it is pulled from the forge; it has to be allowed to cool. When metal is force-cooled rapidly, through a process called "quenching," the result is a very hard but often rather brittle metal. Tempering, on the other hand, allows the material to cool slowly, releasing heat at a natural rate. In the end, the metal is not only strong but also durable. Each means of cooling serves its own purpose in metallurgy, but too often in churches we act as if quenching is the only path to wholeness. We

We release the burden of possibly getting the outcome wrong in a predetermined narrative, and we make ourselves part of a story whose trajectory is ultimately always bent toward redemption.

want those freshly plucked from the refiner's fire to heal quickly and be ready to get to work, when they would likely be better served by a more gradual process that allows them to come to terms with their trauma at their own pace. We must be willing to hold space for grief, processing, and (eventually) recovery, however long it takes, without rushing the hurting individual to "find meaning," as if that will somehow negate everything bad that happened.

The other challenge with the refiner's fire metaphor is that it can be used to place the emphasis of the ordeal on self-improvement— what about *you* needed to be changed. This is not only a round-about form of victim blaming, but it also limits our scope. When we become consumed with asking why this is happening to—or even for—us, we have misaligned our focus. The emphasis should not be on us. Our real questions should be, Why is this happening to/for *the world*? What is my option for choosing grace or healing or betterment? How do I help make the world whole?

If the emphasis is not on how the trial "improves" or "refines" us but instead on how each situation gives us a chance to intro-duce more order or grace or restoration into the world, we are shifting from looking for answers that may never come to look-ing for opportunities to live out our God-given stewardship on this planet. When we stop trying to guess God's endgame, we can create significance in the moment. Rather than feeling trapped by whatever we've decided the allegory must mean, we free our-selves to work in the present—to relieve suffering, to extend grace, to spread love. We release the burden of possibly getting the outcome wrong in a predetermined narrative, and we make ourselves part of a story whose trajectory is ultimately always bent toward redemption.

Why are these awful things happening to me? Sometimes there is no answer, no "because." Some pain cannot be justified by any de-cent reasoning or theology. But despite the evil that exists around us, we still have the option to work toward creating a world that is less broken. Something in creation is out of line, and it's up to you—the beautiful gift of choice—to determine how to respond. We develop mercy, empathy, wisdom, gratefulness—all of which are attributes that point outward in how they impact society as we function as cocreators with or laborers alongside God to restore creation (1 Cor. 3:9). It is the option to choose wholeness over brokenness over and over.

Felicity explains the key role each of us plays in how we can add grace and peace to the world simply by changing the responsibility we take upon ourselves to look out for one another:

> You talk about how people in churches gaslight us in the name of God, but we gaslight him, also. We say we will do one thing with the way we live our lives and then we go out in the world, and that's not at all how we are living. We invite people to church with the promise of it being a loving place, but once we get them there it's "Shame! Shame! Shame!" We spend so much energy telling hurting people, "I'll pray for you," but so often we stop there. Buy them a meal if you can afford it. Ask if they need shelter. Don't tell them there is a reason for whatever they are going through, like they're doing something wrong if they aren't grateful for it. That isn't helping, it's just piling on more shame. Just do something that actually meets a need.

Instead of trying to find meaning, we are given the chance to create it. Allison, who shared about her assault in chapter 6, said something similar: "I don't ever want to put anything good on what happened to me. [The assailant] didn't do me any favors. But I did choose afterward to have more empathy, to be more open-minded and less judgmental, because I understood in a different way that there are hurts and pains real people are going through in the world."

Even the smallest gestures of humanity can help release someone from being retraumatized within a faith system that has already been tested. Chekhov famously wrote, "If in the first act you have hung a pistol on the wall, then in the following one it should be fired. Otherwise don't put it there."[3] In other words, every detail in a story should carry significance, whether literal or symbolic. However, our lives are not literary creations, so we don't have to seek meaning—or demand that anyone else do the same—from our pain. Our lives are not bound by a series of symbolic gestures or metaphorical parallels. As Kurt, whose story was outlined in chapter 5, puts it: "We wrongly attribute meaning to the overall narrative arc instead of being committed to creating meaning day by day. We are commanded to love our neighbor; that's not a narrative but a daily task."

Look at Hebrews 11:39-40 again: "Yet all these, though they were commended for their faith, did not receive what was promised, since God had provided something better so that they would not, apart from us, be made perfect." There was no satisfying ending for those ancient martyrs because their story wasn't over yet; their work was not yet complete. As we each limp toward glory in our own time and place, we are carrying forward the very tools we need to restore a portion of God's creation. We are both the victims and the redeeming hope of a broken world.

Our job is not to put a rosy face on the carnage of other people's sin in our own lives. Our job is not to try to anticipate God's meaning and then manipulate outcomes accordingly at the risk of somehow screwing up the ultimate plan if we end up guessing wrong. Our job is to make meaning of the circumstances. We are entrusted with the sacred responsibility to create order. To defend justice. To restore peace.

Even if we never witness that victory ourselves.

Even if the story ends before the chaos does.

Even if the order is not ours to comprehend.

Even if we are still in the Valley of the Shadow of Death.
Even if we never see Moses plucked from the bulrushes.
Even if the stone has not yet been rolled away from the tomb.
Because the meaning, ultimately, lies not in what happens, but in what we make of it.

14

AUTHENTICITY:
A GOD OF INFINITE FACES

Ezekiel 3:1–21
Acts 2:1–21

W e've all almost certainly heard at least one sermon about
how Ezekiel ate the scroll of the Lord so as to fill his body
with it and then declared, "And in my mouth it was as sweet as
honey" (Ezek. 3:3). But how many sermons have focused on what
follows, after God lays out the seemingly impossible charge to
his prophet to turn the people from their wicked ways? Ezekiel
writes, "The spirit lifted me up and bore me away; *I went in bitterness in the heat of my spirit*, the hand of the LORD being strong
upon me. I came to the exiles at Tel-abib, who lived by the river
Chebar. *And I sat there among them, stunned*, for seven days" (3:14–
15). The NIV interprets the same passage slightly differently: "The
Spirit then lifted me up and took me away, and *I went in bitterness
and in the anger of my spirit*, with the strong hand of the LORD on
me. I came to the exiles who lived at Tel Aviv near the Kebar River.
And there, where they were living, I sat among them for seven
days—*deeply distressed*."

Whatever the translation, the takeaway is still the same: Ezekiel does not accept his burden happily or go forth rejoicing. He

is angry. Bitter. Stunned. Overwhelmed. This is not a portrait of a joyful, eager servant; this is a man overcome with negative emotions and deep despair at what he has been asked to shoulder. But notice what else is true: the "hand of the Lord" is on Ezekiel in strong measure during this time. He is not alone. The Lord's hand may weigh on him heavily, but it does not leave him; if anything, this implies that Ezekiel has an extra measure of the presence of God in his bitterness.

When we only look to the ending of the book of Ezekiel to see what great work God accomplished, we miss the lessons to be gained from the middle part of the story, where the outcome is still unclear. What we see there is one of the greatest prophets in history feeling frustration and anger at his circumstances and at the fact that God seems unwilling to listen to his petitions or objections or to change his circumstances. God allowed Ezekiel to feel bitterness and anger at his commission, sitting for seven days in his "deep distress," so that he would not only have a sense of the profound gravity of his prophetic mission, but also so that he would be more empathetic toward the people to whom he was being sent when he charged them with their offenses against God. They, too, were likely to be bothered by the news imparted to them. Most importantly, however, we see that Ezekiel carried on. God reminds Ezekiel that the weight of the charge has nothing to do with the results and everything to do simply with the execution: "Go to the exiles, to your people, and speak to them. Say to them, 'Thus says the Lord GOD'; *whether they hear or refuse to hear*" (3:11). It can be easy to tie our emotions to the outcome of a struggle, as if the burden becomes even greater if we somehow fail or a satisfying ending is the only part of the story that carries any significance. God's pleasure in Ezekiel had nothing to do with the success or failure of Ezekiel's mission, but only that he carried it out. God didn't tell Ezekiel to "buck up" or "check your attitude, son." God simply told Ezekiel to go and shoulder the load, tackle the challenge, do The Thing—as best he could.

The same is true for us, whether we navigate our pain in such a way that we lead others to Christ through our shining example or we limp our way through and stumble out the other side broken, beaten, but somehow still clinging to the last tattered shreds of faith. Either way, we are still running the race laid out for us, specifically. There are some periods in our lives where we are asked to evangelize and other times when we are asked only to endure. God rarely awards points for style. It may not have been pretty, but Ezekiel modeled incredible strength in his willingness to slog forward. In this way, Ezekiel is a bit like Enos the space chimp we discussed at the opening of the book: he carried on with his mission even when he felt betrayed, injured, and mis-used—but he didn't do so with a placid smile or insincere praise. Ezekiel spoke honestly and authentically both to God and to the readers of his story. Rather than hiding his discontent behind pious words of surrender and submission, he laid all parts bare. Yet still, so many sermons have found a way to skim past that to highlight only the "acceptable" parts of Ezekiel's story—the lines where he rails against sin and the passages that paint a flattering portrait of obedience. The parts that align nicely with the ideals of many modern churches.

Experiencing God authentically means embracing rather than fighting your God-given emotions—coming to God, as the old hymn says, "just as I am." Preachers making altar calls love to declare that the unsaved need not change themselves before approaching the throne of God; why not the same standard for those who believe, or who are trying to believe, or who once be-lieved but are no longer sure?

Allow yourself to acknowledge the hurt, the unfairness, the heartache, the regret, the emptiness, the desperation, the injus-tice, the sheer awfulness of whatever you are experiencing. Speak plainly about your doubts and disappointments, your anxiety and your anger. It might even be worth asking yourself if you had known from the start that God was not going to show up in the way you expected whether it would have changed anything about your journey. Maybe the answer is "absolutely nothing at all," or maybe it's "I'd have done everything differently." Maybe it's somewhere in between. No one else can answer this for you. The point is that it's okay to ask the questions, just as it's okay to admit that maybe your belief structure needs to undergo an audit to see whether you actually still believe all the things in which you've rooted your spiritual identity. It's okay to admit that your current circumstances are maybe not the path of perfect peace we were promised in Isaiah 26:3 or the life of abundance described in John 10:10.

It's also okay to admit that your struggles are legitimate. Just because someone may have it worse than you does not diminish the reality of your own pain. Don't let anyone tell you to snap out of it by counting your blessings. As the saying goes, "It doesn't matter if you drown in seven feet of water or in seventy. You've still drowned." You don't need to downplay your own circumstances just because they aren't as drastic as someone else's. In the same way, it's easy to compare your faith response to others who seem to accept their struggles with so much more peace and trust than you have. You may feel jealous of them, or even angry that they are able to bear up so much more gracefully than you are. But their relationship with God is not yours, nor are their burdens the same as yours. Don't forget that Ezekiel shows us that an unhappy, conflict-filled response is every bit as "biblical" as a temperate, grace-filled one.

Consider Isaiah 5:20, which decries those

> who call evil good
> and good evil,
> who put darkness for light
> and light for darkness,
> who put bitter for sweet
> and sweet for bitter!

Usually, that Scripture is used to condemn those who take something immoral and raise it up for the sake of justifying their own desires, but we need to consider it in reverse, too. The word translated as "evil" here is one of the most commonly used words in the Hebrew Scriptures to mean anything negative, bad, harmful, misery-inducing, ugly, or even sad. Likewise, the root word translated as "good" means not just "morally upright" but anything pleasant, agreeable, or even beautiful. This verse in Isaiah isn't simply condemning the justification of sin for selfish reasons; it is also warning against declaring anything difficult, unpleasant, or hurtful to be lovely and pleasurable—which is exactly what we do when we pretend our relationship with God is hunky-dory despite inward spiritual turmoil. Be wary of those who might shame you for not facing your trials with more joy. You don't have to pretend that you are happy; you shouldn't have to lie to be a "good Christian."

Don't force yourself to see a silver lining. Don't manufacture a happy ending because you think that's what you're supposed to do or because you might impact your witness or out of fear that you could somehow damage God's "image" or "brand" to outsiders. Don't pretend to be placid, calm, and gladly accepting your circumstances when you're not. To do so

> *You don't have to pretend that you are happy; you shouldn't have to lie to be a "good Christian."*

is to shortchange what you are actually feeling right now, in this moment. Let things be what they are instead of believing you must somehow spin them into something acceptable for your church. *Sometimes things really are every bit as bad as you think they are.* Allow yourself to sit in the pain, the brokenness, the unfairness of it for a while. Allow yourself to experience it for what it is instead of what you feel you have to try to make it, how you should justify it, the ways you want to fix it, or how you want to project it onto some hypothetical future scenario where it is all part of an inevitably happy outcome. If those realizations and connections come in the future, let them come organically and celebrate them if they do. But don't force them. Don't try to convince yourself of something. Don't try to pretend you're okay when you're not. Don't try to put a good face on something awful because you think that is what your Christian testimony requires. Nowhere does God ask us to be dishonest to protect the divine reputation for outsiders. God does not need us to lie, nor does the Almighty need a PR agent to spin a shiny gospel to the world. God *does* need us to be honest and relational.

Own your story. Live in it. Inhabit that space. Let it be part—though not the only part—of who you are, how you grew into that person, and who you are still becoming. The events in your life are yours to make sense of as you will, without the burdens or shame or inhibitions others might want you to feel. Don't believe you have to stay silent to protect someone else's reputation. As Guggenheim Fellow and famed author Anne Lamott brilliantly remarked, "You own everything that happened to you. Tell your stories. If people wanted you to write warmly about them, they should have behaved better."[1]

There is another significant challenge, though, when your story is not entirely your own—and most of your stories rarely are. What do you do when your own battle with depression is informed by the state of your partner's mental health? What do you choose to speak about publicly when a friend's addiction has hurt you? How do you deal with your own pain when your child is overcoming trauma? How much do you share when details about your pain could injure an innocent party? How can you be fully authentic when your story is not wholly yours to tell? Sometimes we must choose between being wholly authentic and keeping a little back because we do not have

Authenticity doesn't mean wanton sharing about personal details or spreading gossip disguised as prayer requests; it means relating to God the way you best connect with the Almighty.

a right to share the pain of others. In that case, it is important to remember that privacy and secrecy are not the same thing. Secrecy implies shame or intentional hiding so as not to be found out. Privacy, on the other hand, implies purposeful guarding of healthy boundaries.

And beyond the confines of privacy for other people, there are also boundaries you may wish to maintain for yourself, even as you practice authentic spiritual engagement with your faith community. Some people seem to share their pain as if it were a badge of honor; they are no more authentic, however, than those who keep it between themselves and God. To some, sharing pain may be liberating; to others, a feeling of sacredness or ownership is protected and preserved when pain is kept close to the vest. Authenticity doesn't mean wanton disclosing of personal details or spreading gossip disguised as prayer requests; it means relating to God the way you best connect with the Almighty.

There are critics who will argue that this is just catering to a self-centered theology, where we put ourselves and what we want at the center of our faith, rather than God. But such centering is inevitable; we are the main character in each of our own lives. This isn't arrogance, it's simply reality. We must approach the old adage "More of God and less of me" with caution. More of *whose version* of God? Are we being asked to suppress sacred, divinely created parts of ourselves for the sake of conforming to someone else's interpretation of what the gospel looks like? How is "death to self" noble when God created and blessed the very self we are trying to suppress? "More of God and less of me" doesn't mean that you slowly choke out parts of yourself until you've extinguished the flame of who the Holy Spirit is calling you to be.

"More of God and less of me" doesn't mean that you slowly choke out parts of yourself until you've extinguished the flame of who the Holy Spirit is calling you to be.

In biology, epigenetics is the study of how inherited genes manifest themselves within a species to account for variation.

The DNA sequence remains the same, but the way that certain traits show up within each individual organism can be vastly different. On an even simpler scale, each person can react differently to allergens, environmental factors, and even stress. If we acknowledge that bodies react differently due to chemistry, and brains process input and experiences differently, why does it seem a stretch to consider that the Holy Spirit might interact differently with each of us as well?

Consider the account of Pentecost in Acts 2. When a crowd of Jesus's followers were all gathered together,

> Suddenly from heaven there came a sound like the rush of a violent wind, and it filled the entire house where they were sitting. Divided tongues, as of fire, appeared among them, and a tongue rested on each of them. All of them were filled with the Holy Spirit and began to speak in other languages, as the Spirit gave them ability.
>
> Now there were devout Jews from every nation under heaven living in Jerusalem. And at this sound the crowd gathered and was bewildered, because each one heard them speaking in the native language of each. Amazed and astonished, they asked, "Are not all these who are speaking Galileans? And how is it that we hear, each of us, in our own native language? Parthians, Medes, Elamites, and residents of Mesopotamia, Judea and Cappadocia, Pontus and Asia, Phrygia and Pamphylia, Egypt and the parts of Libya belonging to Cyrene, and visitors from Rome, both Jews and proselytes, Cretans and Arabs—in our own languages we hear them speaking about God's deeds of power." All were amazed and perplexed, saying to one another, "What does this mean?" But others sneered and said, "They are filled with new wine." (2:2-13)

Just like Jesus's followers at Pentecost, what we hear—the message of the law or the words of the gospel—is the same. But *how* we hear it—the way we experience God—will vary as it is translated into the form that impacts each person most. Don't feel you must strain your ears to try to understand what God is saying to someone else. There will always be detractors, critics, and scoffers who want to discount or disparage anyone who encounters God differently; that is their issue, not yours.

Authenticity means recognizing the Almighty as God has made God's self known to us both through Scripture and through experience. It means that we refuse any longer to allow anyone to shame us for our honesty—like those who interpret Hebrews 4:12 a little too literally, gladly wielding the Word of God as a "two-edged sword" of their own agenda, leaving people bloodied and battered in the name of righteousness. They seem to forget that sword they swing so gladly is also "able to judge the thoughts and intentions of the heart." God knows your heart. God knows your motivations and provocations. God knows why you hurt and what is causing you to wrestle. God knows how you were made and how God has chosen to make God's own self known to you, personally. God also knows when God's Word is twisted by those who are driven by close-mindedness, exclusion, legalism, or power.

> *Don't feel you must strain your ears to try to understand what God is saying to someone else.*

Even so, "just be authentic" may still feel like a pat response. Of course God knows your heart, but that doesn't change your circumstances. It doesn't take away the trauma or the heartbreak or the uncertainty. It doesn't soothe the anger or undo the abuse or answer the questions. It doesn't give you the relief you plead for or stop the tears you are pouring out at God's feet. It doesn't change the fact that sometimes the faith community that was supposed to walk with you through your earthly trials rejects you, shies away, shuts down, or closes you out because your authenticity was too much for them.

So where is the plot twist there? Where is God stepping in with the perfect solution to save the day just as it seems all hope is gone? Honestly, there is no easy answer for that—and we should be leery of anyone who suggests otherwise. The truth is, sometimes there is no flipping the script; no reframing the narrative; no reinterpreting the old, familiar Scriptures; and no eleventh-hour miracle. There is no new perspective to consider or hackneyed metaphors about looking at life through a microscope while God uses a telescope or turning the tapestry around to see the finished side instead of the knotted and tangled one. Those approaches are available in any Christian study on pain and suffering; there is nothing new this book can offer. This study is intended to speak the unspeakable things, to give voice to the feelings we've too often been taught to ignore, deny, dismiss, or smooth over. As Paul wrote in 1 Corinthians: "My speech and my proclamation were not with plausible words of wisdom, but with a demonstration of the Spirit and of power, so that your faith might rest not on human wisdom but on the power of God" (2:4–5). Our faith should not rest in interpretations forced upon us by people in power but in how we perceive and recognize the ways that God works in and through us.

There is irony in the fact that, as we come to know God better, we may actually consciously think about God less. It may not mean that our faith is slipping or our belief is becoming lazy or complacent, but rather, that as we become more and more God-infused in our daily lives, we no longer have to bring God consciously to mind as often in order to feel God's presence. We no longer have to hold up our WWJD? bracelet as the lens through which every choice must be deliberately filtered, because the spirit of Christ makes such a filter automatic. As a friend of mine observed, maybe it's a bit like dancing: at some point, the movements become so natural that you no longer have to stop and think about each one you learned in class, but simply put them together to move in time with the music as it changes.

This is the real challenge facing all believers as we seek to reconcile Scripture with experience. We have been trained to ask,

"What does the Bible say about that?"—and the impulse is a good one. The problem arises when we stop there, as if the Bible is the only way that God speaks to us and is an ironclad guarantee of exactly how things will go. When we slap Scriptures on a situation without considering the broader context of the verses or the individual's traumas or background, and then use those verses to dismiss someone's experiences, we are limiting God—hemming in the Creator of the universe with God's own sacred text. We are saying, in effect, "God is only as big as these verses." This is not to say that we ought to toss out or disregard the Bible; it is merely reclaiming it from those who would use it to dismiss, tear down, or invalidate.

We must remember that the Bible is sacred because it is our *introduction* to God; it is not the end point of our understanding. The Bible was never intended to create boundaries for God; let us not limit the Creator of the universe with God's own set of Scriptures. When we act as if the expansiveness of God can be contained within sixty-six books, we are shortchanging both God and ourselves.

An infinite God is going to have some facets that do not seem consistent with our limited human capacity for understanding. Rather than trying to explain these away or pretending they don't exist, we can look to Scripture to see how God acted—or didn't—contrary to our expectations, and what that can mean—or not—for us.

In Revelation 4, we are given a glimpse into the throne room of God, where seraphim cry "Holy, holy, holy" continually as they gaze upon God. These creatures, "covered with eyes, in front and in back," declare the divinity of God with each new divine facet they behold as they view him from myriad angles. Who are we to say every single face is one that we can discern in the pages of the Bible? We must reevaluate how we understand, accept, and work alongside an often-inscrutable God as "joint heirs with Christ" (Rom. 8:17).

It can be intimidating to take the first steps toward freeing ourselves from the limited view of God we may have been taught we must uphold in order to remain in our "faith tribe." God does not gaslight us; human beings do, and they often do so in God's name through a selective, incomplete, myopic, or power-driven agenda. When Holy Scriptures and toxic authoritativeness are used to harm or control people earnestly seeking truth, we must take whatever steps are necessary to stop the abuse and provide a path toward the health and safety of the victims. James writes, "For just as the body without the spirit is dead, so faith without works is also dead" (James 2:26). We have a divine duty to take action. We have a right to encounter God where we are. We have a sacred responsibility to experience God authentically.

DISCUSSION QUESTIONS

Introduction
This Is Not a Book about That

The book opens with a story about Enos the space chimp. How do you see Enos's story in relation to your own faith? Talk about times when you have felt anger toward God and didn't know what to do with it.

What are you looking for in reading this book? What compelled you to start reading it?

Chapter 1
Shell-Shocked Faith: Reconciling Scripture and Experience

This chapter discusses how Jesus asked his apostles to use their experience to name who he is. What are some other examples of how Jesus used experience rather than religious doctrine to point to truth?

If the Bible is the beginning but not the end of how we come to know God, what are other ways to experience God?

This chapter compares shell-shocked soldiers of World War I to Christians who have suffered in life and how the Bible or their view of God doesn't match their experiences. How can you better provide help for those with spiritual shell shock? Have you ever experienced this yourself?

Chapter 2
Asking: The God Who Demands Too Much

Read all of Job chapter 13. Then describe your thoughts as you react to Job's emotional words toward God and toward fellow believers.

In this chapter, the author looks toward the Old Testament and Jewish practices of debating and wrestling with Holy Scriptures. Why do you think Christian theology has lost or de-emphasized the questioning of Scripture or of God's motives?

What would you consider the more public or acceptable forms of grief, and what are ones that our society downplays? Why do we do this?

Why do some churches and religious traditions treat certain emotions, such as sadness, differently from others, such as positivity?

Chapter 3
Apathy: The God Who Doesn't Seem to Care

Read Luke 10:38–42 through a lens of Martha doing ministry rather than household chores. How does this reading change the context of Martha's questions to Jesus and his answers to her?

When have you experienced the absence of God? If you've never experienced it, how do you respond to God in your daily life? If you have experienced times where you felt God didn't care, what did you do?

Have you ever considered the idea that God's absence in our suffering might stem from divine reminders that God is not the source of suffering? How does that idea feel?

What have your big emotions taught you about communicating with God?

Chapter 4
Atrophy: The God Who Can't Seem to Act

Has there been a time in your life where God seemed inactive? Describe your thoughts and feelings during this time.

Have you ever wondered why Jesus didn't heal everyone at the pool of Bethesda? How do you view God's role in healing?

After reading this chapter, how might you shift your lens with regard to suffering, working hard, and rewards in relation to others?

Chapter 5
Anger: The God of Punishment

The chapter discusses the story of Achan and his family being stoned to death after the fall of Jericho. What are other passages in the Bible that are hard to understand or accept, especially with regard to how we view God?

This chapter serves as a "what not to do" when other people are suffering. What are things we could say instead to other believers who are suffering with an illness, a loss, or another hardship?

Read through Romans 14. What are areas in your life where you have projected your own shortcomings, condemned others, or acted out in anger toward other people's sins? How might you handle that differently in the future?

Chapter 6
Ambiguity: *The God of the Inscrutable*

What are some examples of legalism from your own life?

How can perfectionism hamper our relationship with God?

The stories presented from the Bible—Jonah, Uzzah, Jael, Abigail, Abraham and Sarah—can offer a view of God that seems confusing or impossible to predict. How can we read these stories with different eyes?

Chapter 7
Abandonment: *The God Who No Longer Feels Present*

How has your image of God changed because of your life's circumstances?

Why do people of faith tend to push back when others question God's presence?

What are some ways that can help lead us back to the source when our questioning seems unanswered?

Chapter 8
Absence: *The God Who Never Was*

Why do people in the Christian community often shun those who have doubts about God?

Do you have relationships with atheists or agnostics? If so, how would you characterize their relationship with faith?

How does the concept of grace and love fit in with the ideas of belief and doubt?

Chapter 9
Arbitrariness: The God of Shifting Goalposts

Have you ever encountered that opening phrase, "God cares more about your holiness than your happiness"? How does the concept of *pikuach nefesh*, or "saving a life," negate this idea?

Where are places in your life that you need to prioritize healthiness over holiness or happiness?

Use the Jane Eyre Decision-Making Flow Chart on page 147 to make a choice you have been avoiding.

Read the account of Abraham and Sarah in Genesis 22:1–23:3. Sarah lived apart from Abraham at the end of her life. What might have been her reasons? How does this story fit into the chapter's theme of healthiness, holiness, and happiness?

Chapter 10
Antagonism: The God of Chaos

How can we actively find a community to help make order out of the chaos in our lives—either through our own mistakes or through unfortunate circumstances?

What are chaotic situations from your past that need forgiveness—lifting the burden of guilt like Cain or purging them like Esau?

This chapter shows that God eventually granted favor to Cain and Esau (the "antagonists" of the story) just as God did for Abel and Jacob. How might seeing these two men in a different light change how you see yourself in relation to God?

Chapter 11
Accountability: The God Who Expects Us to Act

How is defiance a part of the gospel?

How is turning the other cheek an act of defiance?

Read Isaiah 58. How are God's people called to act? How do you see the modern church meeting or missing the criteria outlined here for "true fasting"?

Where are places of injustice that you feel called to step in, acting as Christ did, to provide grace and mercy, strength and influence, allyship and solidarity? What are some things that may keep people of faith from taking action?

Chapter 12
Anxiety and Abuse: The God of Manipulation

If you struggle with spiritual anxiety, how do you feel this colors the way you perceive God? If not, consider whether you know anyone who does seem to have this kind of anxiety. How might this impact their relationship with God or even their day-to-day life? What can you do to respond with love or support?

Have you ever struggled with loving yourself? What are your reactions to reading the passage about Jesus and his two commands—that "loving our neighbors is on the same footing as loving God"?

Based on Courtney and Mike's story of spiritual abuse within a Christian organization, what might be some signs you would recognize as spiritual abuse?

What are steps you can take to love yourself better as a person of inherent worth?

Chapter 13
Allegory: The God Who Must Fit Our Narrative

How do the differing perceptions of time between ancient Greek and ancient Jewish cultures help you to reflect on your own life?

Is there a narrative arc in your life that needs reshaping? Are you assigning meaning to something that God may not have assigned? What are some memories, events, losses, or hurts you've experienced in your past that seem meaningless?

What are some circumstances you may have tried to manipulate in order to achieve the outcome you thought God wanted? Have you ever tried to read God's will onto your own to justify your actions?

How can your past hurts or struggles be used to better shape the world around you?

Chapter 14
Authenticity: A God of Infinite Faces

After reading through this entire book, what does authenticity look like for your personal faith?

Has your view or understanding of God shifted at all?

How might God use your own specific talents, gifts, and past experiences to help others and connect more closely to God?

End of Book Discussion

What surprised you most about the book?

What do you not want to forget after reading this book?

What chapter challenged your current mind-set most? What chapter was the most uplifting for you?

NOTES

Introduction

1. James P. Henry, MD, PhD, and John D. Mosely, DMV, eds., *Results of the Project Mercury Basllistic and Orbital Chimpansee Flights* (prepared by Manned Spacecraft Center, Houston, TX, Office of Scientific and Technical Information, National Aeronautics and Space Administration, Washington, DC, 1963), 51, 54.

Chapter 1

1. Carlos Baker, *Hemingway: The Writer as Artist*, 4th ed. (Princeton: Princeton University Press, 1972), 80–81.

2. Unless otherwise indicated, scriptural quotations come from the New Revised Standard Version.

3. For a more in-depth discussion of this phenomenon, see Allyson Chiu's article "Time to Ditch 'Toxic Positivity,' Experts Say: 'It's Okay Not to Be Okay,'" *Washington Post*, August 19, 2020.

4. Check out A. J. Jacobs, *The Year of Living Biblically* (New York: Simon & Schuster, 2007), and Rachel Held Evans, *The Year of Biblical Womanhood* (Nashville: Nelson, 2012).

5. This is not a newfangled, postmodern approach. Richard Hooker, a prominent sixth-century theologian, proposed a triumvirate of Scripture, tradition, and reason for spiritual discernment. This system, later dubbed the "three-legged stool" of Anglicanism, inspired other religious thinkers to create similar methods, such as the Wesleyan Quadrilateral (Scripture, tradition, reason, and experience) and Richard Rohr's more recent metaphor of a tricycle consisting of tradition, Scripture, and experience.

Chapter 2

1. Names and, in some cases, identifying details of those who offered testimonials in this book have been changed.

2. Jenni Frazer, "Wiesel: Yes, We Really Did Put God on Trial," *Jewish Chronicle*, September 19, 2008, https://www.thejc.com/news/uk/wiesel-yes-we-really-did-put-god-on-trial-1.5056.

Chapter 4

1. All quotations from Porphyry come from *Porphyry's "Against the Christians": The Literary Remains*, ed. and trans. R. Joseph Hoffmann (Amherst, NY: Prometheus Books, 1994).

Chapter 6

1. For further study on this point, including broader applications, consider many of the insightful books and articles by the Reverend Wilda C. Gafney, PhD, including *Womanist Midrash: A Reintroduction*

to the *Women of the Torah and the Throne* (Louisville: Westminster John Knox, 2017).

Chapter 11

1. John Hospers, *An Introduction to Philosophical Analysis*, 3rd ed. (London: Routledge, 1990), 310.

2. Most notably, perhaps, Walter Wink and Amy-Jill Levine. While interpretations of the significance of these passages vary, the general consensus is that they were not intended as instruction to subject one's self to abuse or injustice as a means of pleasing God.

Chapter 12

1. Thomas A. Santa, CSsR, *Understanding Scrupulosity: Questions, Helps, and Encouragement* (Liguori, MO: Liguori Publications, 2007), is a brilliant and highly accessible guide to approaching this issue, no matter what branch of Christianity the reader follows.

2. Flavil Yeakly, *The Discipling Dilemma*, 2nd ed. (Nashville: Gospel Advocate, 1988), 46–47.

3. Gary W. Hartz and Henry C. Everett, "Fundamentalist Religion and Its Effect on Mental Health," *Journal of Religion and Health* 28, no. 3 (Fall 1989): 207, 210.

Chapter 13

1. Special thanks to Dr. Cheryl Durham, Pauline scholar at Master's International University of Divinity, for the rowing metaphor and for explaining this complex topic in simple terms.

2. C. S. Lewis, "The World's Last Night," in *The World's Last Night and Other Essays* (New York: Harcourt Brace, 1960).

3. Ernest J. Simmons, *Chekhov: A Biography* (Chicago: University of Chicago Press, 1962), 190.

Chapter 14

1. TED Talk by Anne Lamott, 12 Truths I Learned from Life and Writing, April 28, 2017, www.ted.com/talks/anne_lamott_12_truths_i _learned_from_life_and_writing.

SCRIPTURE INDEX